Mediterranean Refresh Cookbook

365-Day Delicious, Healthy and Fresh Recipes for Living

Your Best Life.

Cecelia Spradley

Table of Contents

INTRODUCTION

The Mediterranean Refresh diet is a variation of the Mediterranean diet that emphasizes consuming whole, minimally processed foods that are rich in nutrients. The Mediterranean diet is based on the traditional foods and eating patterns of countries surrounding the Mediterranean Sea, such as Greece, Italy, and Spain. The Mediterranean Refresh diet includes some additional features, such as eating more plant-based foods, incorporating lean proteins, reducing processed foods, limiting red meat, and incorporating healthy fats.

The Mediterranean Refresh diet is a well-balanced, nutrient-dense eating pattern that can help support long-term health and wellbeing. Research has shown that following a Mediterranean diet may reduce the risk of chronic diseases, such as heart disease, diabetes, and certain types of cancer. The Mediterranean diet has also been associated with improved brain function, lower inflammation, and improved gut health.

One of the key features of the Mediterranean Refresh diet is the emphasis on consuming a variety of colorful fruits and vegetables. Fruits and vegetables are rich in vitamins, minerals, fiber, and antioxidants that can help support overall health and wellbeing. Research has shown that consuming a diet rich in fruits and vegetables may help reduce the risk of chronic diseases, such as heart disease and cancer.

Another key feature of the Mediterranean Refresh diet is the inclusion of lean protein sources like seafood, poultry, and eggs in moderation. Seafood, in particular, is rich in omega-3 fatty acids, which have been shown to have anti-inflammatory properties and may help reduce the risk of heart disease. Consuming lean protein sources can also help support muscle growth and repair.

The Mediterranean Refresh diet also emphasizes reducing processed and packaged foods. Processed and packaged foods are often high in added sugars, unhealthy fats, and salt, which can contribute to the development of chronic diseases. Instead, the Mediterranean Refresh diet encourages consuming whole, minimally processed foods that are rich in nutrients and can help support overall health and wellbeing.

In addition to reducing processed foods, the Mediterranean Refresh diet recommends limiting red meat consumption. Red meat is often high in saturated fat and has been associated with an increased risk of chronic diseases, such as heart disease and cancer. Instead, the Mediterranean Refresh diet encourages consuming lean protein sources like seafood, poultry, and eggs.

The Mediterranean Refresh diet also emphasizes incorporating healthy fats like olive oil and nuts. Healthy fats are important for overall health and can help reduce the risk of chronic diseases. Olive oil, in particular, is rich in monounsaturated fats and has been associated with improved heart health.

While the Mediterranean Refresh diet can offer a wide range of benefits, it's important to note that everyone's dietary needs and preferences are unique. Some people may find it challenging to follow this eating pattern, especially if they are used to consuming a lot of processed foods or meat.

Additionally, it's important to remember that following any specific diet alone may not be enough to achieve optimal health. Exercise, stress management, and getting enough sleep are also important factors that contribute to overall wellbeing.

If you're interested in following the Mediterranean Refresh diet, it's important to work with a registered dietitian or healthcare provider to ensure that your individual nutrient needs are being met. They can also help you develop a customized meal plan that aligns with your goals and lifestyle.

In conclusion, the Mediterranean Refresh diet is a healthy and sustainable eating pattern that can offer a wide range of health benefits. By emphasizing whole, minimally processed foods and healthy fats, individuals can support their overall health and wellbeing while enjoying a delicious and satisfying diet.

Fundamentals of Mediterranean Refresh diet

The Mediterranean Refresh diet is based on the traditional eating patterns of countries bordering the Mediterranean Sea, such as Greece, Italy, and Spain. The diet emphasizes a plant-based, whole foods approach to eating, with an emphasis on healthy fats and limited consumption of animal products. Here are some of the key fundamentals of the Mediterranean Refresh diet:

Emphasis on plant-based foods: The Mediterranean Refresh diet emphasizes the consumption of whole, minimally processed plant foods like fruits, vegetables, whole grains, legumes, nuts, and seeds. These foods are rich in fiber, vitamins, minerals, and antioxidants, which can help support overall health and wellbeing.

Healthy fats: The Mediterranean Refresh diet emphasizes the consumption of healthy fats, like olive oil, nuts, seeds, and avocado. These fats are rich in monounsaturated and polyunsaturated fatty acids, which can help support heart health, reduce inflammation, and promote satiety.

Limited animal products: While the Mediterranean Refresh diet is not strictly vegetarian or vegan, it does limit the consumption of animal products, particularly red meat. Fish and poultry are consumed in moderation, while plant-based proteins like tofu, tempeh, and seitan are encouraged.

Whole grains: The Mediterranean Refresh diet encourages the consumption of whole grains, like brown rice, quinoa, and whole wheat bread. These grains are rich in fiber, vitamins, and minerals, and can help support digestive health and reduce the risk of chronic disease.

Mindful eating: The Mediterranean Refresh diet emphasizes the importance of mindful eating, including paying attention to hunger and fullness cues, enjoying food in a relaxed environment, and savoring the flavors and textures of foods.

Social and environmental responsibility: The Mediterranean Refresh diet places emphasis on social and environmental responsibility, encouraging the consumption of locally-sourced, organic, and sustainably-produced foods whenever possible.

Herbs and spices: The Mediterranean Refresh diet emphasizes the use of herbs and spices to flavor foods instead of relying on salt. This can help reduce the intake of sodium, which is important for maintaining healthy blood pressure levels.

Red wine in moderation: The Mediterranean Refresh diet allows for the consumption of red wine in moderation, typically one glass per day for women and two glasses per day for men. Red wine is rich in antioxidants and has been shown to have beneficial effects on heart health.

Family-style dining: In many Mediterranean cultures, meals are often enjoyed in a family-style setting, with multiple dishes shared among the group. This encourages a social and relaxed atmosphere, which can support mindful eating and overall enjoyment of food.

Physical activity: The Mediterranean Refresh diet emphasizes the importance of physical activity for overall health and wellbeing. Regular exercise, such as walking, swimming, or cycling, is encouraged as a part of a healthy lifestyle.

By emphasizing whole, minimally processed plant foods, healthy fats, and mindful eating, the Mediterranean Refresh diet can support overall health and wellbeing in a sustainable and delicious way.

Let's dive a bit deeper into the benefits of the Mediterranean Refresh diet

Reduced Risk of Chronic Diseases

One of the primary benefits of the Mediterranean Refresh diet is its potential to reduce the risk of chronic diseases, such as heart disease, diabetes, and certain types of cancer. Research has shown that following a Mediterranean diet may help improve blood sugar control, reduce inflammation, and improve cholesterol levels, all of which can contribute to a lower risk of chronic diseases.

Improved Brain Function

The Mediterranean diet has also been associated with improved brain function. A study published in the Journal of the American Medical Association found that older adults who followed a Mediterranean diet had better cognitive function over a three-year period than those who did not follow the diet. Additionally, the Mediterranean diet has been associated with a reduced risk of developing Alzheimer's disease and other forms of dementia.

Lower Inflammation

Inflammation is a natural response of the body's immune system, but chronic inflammation can contribute to the development of chronic diseases. The Mediterranean diet, which emphasizes consuming anti-inflammatory foods like fruits, vegetables, whole grains, and healthy fats, has been shown to help reduce inflammation in the body.

Improved Gut Health

May improve mood: The Mediterranean Refresh diet is rich in omega-3 fatty acids and other nutrients that have been linked to improved mood and reduced risk of depression. Additionally, this eating pattern emphasizes whole, nutrient-dense foods that can help promote feelings of wellbeing and satisfaction.

Supports healthy aging: The Mediterranean Refresh diet is rich in antioxidants and anti-inflammatory compounds that can help reduce the risk of age-related diseases and support healthy aging. Additionally, this eating pattern emphasizes whole, minimally processed foods that can help promote overall health and wellbeing as individuals age.

May improve fertility: The Mediterranean Refresh diet is rich in nutrients that have been linked to improved fertility, such as folate, iron, and zinc. Additionally, this eating pattern emphasizes whole, nutrient-dense foods that can help support overall reproductive health.

Sustainable and environmentally friendly: The Mediterranean Refresh diet emphasizes whole, plant-based foods and minimizes the consumption of animal products, which can help reduce the environmental impact of food production. Additionally, this eating pattern emphasizes local and seasonal foods, which can further reduce the environmental impact of food production and support sustainable agriculture.

Improves cognitive function: The Mediterranean Refresh diet is rich in nutrients that have been shown to support cognitive function, such as omega-3 fatty acids and B vitamins. Additionally, this eating pattern may help reduce the risk of cognitive decline and dementia in older adults.

May reduce the risk of type 2 diabetes: The Mediterranean Refresh diet is rich in whole, minimally processed foods that are naturally low in added sugars and refined carbohydrates, which can help reduce the risk of developing type 2 diabetes. Additionally, this eating pattern emphasizes healthy fats, such as olive oil and nuts, which have been shown to improve insulin sensitivity.

May support healthy skin: The Mediterranean Refresh diet is rich in nutrients and antioxidants that can help support healthy skin, such as vitamin C and vitamin E. Additionally, this eating pattern emphasizes whole, minimally processed foods that can help reduce the risk of skin damage and premature aging.

May improve sleep quality: The Mediterranean Refresh diet is rich in nutrients that have been linked to improved sleep quality, such as magnesium and B vitamins. Additionally, this eating pattern emphasizes whole, minimally processed foods that can help promote feelings of relaxation and wellbeing, which may support better sleep.

May improve athletic performance: The Mediterranean Refresh diet is rich in nutrients that can help support athletic performance, such as carbohydrates for energy and protein for muscle repair and growth. Additionally, this eating pattern emphasizes whole, minimally processed foods that can help reduce inflammation and promote overall health and wellbeing, which may support better athletic performance.

Overall, the Mediterranean Refresh diet offers a wide range of benefits for overall health, wellbeing, and the environment. By emphasizing whole, nutrient-dense foods and minimizing the consumption of processed and animal-based foods, individuals can support their overall health while also promoting sustainability and environmental stewardship.

Mediterranean Refresh diet Allow Food

- Fruits: apples, oranges, berries, bananas, grapes, pears, peaches, and more.

- Vegetables: spinach, kale, broccoli, tomatoes, cucumbers, carrots, eggplant, zucchini, and more.

- Whole grains: oats, quinoa, brown rice, barley, bulgur, farro, and more.

- Legumes: chickpeas, lentils, kidney beans, black beans, and more.

- Nuts and seeds: almonds, cashews, walnuts, pumpkin seeds, chia seeds, and more.

- Healthy fats: olive oil, avocado, olives, nuts, and seeds.

- Seafood: salmon, tuna, sardines, shrimp, and more.

- Poultry: chicken and turkey.

- Dairy: yogurt, cheese, and milk.

- Herbs and spices: garlic, basil, oregano, rosemary, thyme, and more.

While this list is not exhaustive, it provides an overview of the types of foods that are allowed on the Mediterranean Refresh diet. It's important to note that while red meat and processed foods are allowed in moderation, the focus of this eating pattern is on whole, nutrient-dense foods.

Mediterranean Refresh diet not allow food

While the Mediterranean Refresh diet emphasizes a wide range of nutrient-dense foods, there are some foods that are limited or not allowed on this eating pattern. Here are some examples:

Processed foods: Highly processed foods, such as chips, candy, and sugary drinks, are generally not allowed on the Mediterranean Refresh diet.

Refined grains: Refined grains, such as white bread and pasta, are limited on the Mediterranean Refresh diet in favor of whole grains.

Red meat: While red meat is not completely eliminated on the Mediterranean Refresh diet, it is limited in favor of seafood, poultry, legumes, and other protein sources.

Added sugars: Added sugars, such as those found in soda and baked goods, are limited on the Mediterranean Refresh diet in favor of naturally occurring sugars found in fruits and other whole foods.

Saturated and trans fats: Saturated and trans fats, which are found in many processed and fast foods, are limited on the Mediterranean Refresh diet in favor of healthy fats, such as those found in nuts, seeds, and olive oil.

While these foods are limited on the Mediterranean Refresh diet, it's important to note that moderation is key. Occasional indulgences are allowed on this eating pattern, as long as they are balanced with a predominantly nutrient-dense diet.

Practical Tips for Following the Mediterranean Refresh Diet

- If you're interested in following the Mediterranean Refresh diet, there are a few practical tips that can help you get started:

- Emphasize whole, minimally processed foods: Focus on consuming a variety of colorful fruits and vegetables, whole grains, legumes, nuts, seeds, and healthy fats like olive oil.

- Incorporate lean proteins: Choose lean protein sources like seafood, poultry, and eggs in moderation.

- Limit processed foods: Avoid processed and packaged foods, such as pre-made meals, sugary drinks, and snacks, as much as possible.

- Limit red meat: Consume red meat occasionally in small portions, and choose lean cuts when possible.

- Experiment with herbs and spices: Use herbs and spices to flavor your food instead of relying on salt or processed sauces.

- Enjoy meals with others: The Mediterranean diet emphasizes enjoying meals with others, so make an effort to share meals with friends and family.

- Stay active: Incorporate physical activity into your daily routine, such as walking, cycling, or swimming.

Here are some additional points to consider when thinking about the Mediterranean Refresh diet:

Variety is key: The Mediterranean Refresh diet emphasizes a wide variety of whole, minimally processed foods, including fruits, vegetables, whole grains, legumes, nuts, seeds, and healthy fats. Eating a variety of different foods can help ensure that you are getting a wide range of nutrients and antioxidants to support overall health and wellbeing.

Lifestyle factors matter: While diet is an important part of overall health, it is not the only factor to consider. Engaging in regular physical activity, managing stress, getting adequate sleep, and avoiding smoking and excessive alcohol consumption are also important factors that can contribute to overall health and wellbeing.

Quality matters: When following the Mediterranean Refresh diet, it is important to focus on the quality of the foods you are eating. Choosing organic, locally-sourced, and sustainably-produced foods whenever possible can help support both your own health and the health of the planet.

Mindful eating is important: Eating mindfully, paying attention to hunger and fullness cues, and enjoying your food in a relaxed and peaceful environment can help promote feelings of satisfaction and wellbeing, while also reducing the risk of overeating and weight gain.

Consulting with a healthcare provider or registered dietitian can be helpful: If you are interested in following the Mediterranean Refresh diet, it can be helpful to consult with a healthcare provider or registered dietitian to ensure that you are meeting your nutrient needs and to discuss any health concerns or questions you may have.

Who should avoid the Mediterranean Refresh diet

The Mediterranean Refresh diet is generally considered to be a healthy and balanced approach to eating, and may be suitable for most people. However, there are some individuals who may need to exercise caution or avoid the diet altogether. Here are some examples:

- **People with allergies or intolerances:** If you have a food allergy or intolerance to any of the foods commonly consumed on the Mediterranean Refresh diet, such as nuts, seafood, or gluten, you may need to modify the diet to meet your specific needs.

- **Individuals with certain medical conditions:** If you have a medical condition that requires a specialized diet, such as diabetes, celiac disease, or kidney disease, you should consult with a healthcare professional before starting the Mediterranean Refresh diet.

- **Pregnant or breastfeeding women:** Pregnant or breastfeeding women mayneed to modify the Mediterranean Refresh diet to ensure adequate intake of key nutrients like calcium, iron, and folate. It is recommended to consult with a healthcare professional to ensure that nutrient needs are being met during pregnancy and breastfeeding.

- **People with a history of disordered eating:** The emphasis on mindful eating and enjoyment of food in the Mediterranean Refresh diet can be beneficial for those with a history of disordered eating. However, it may not be suitable for all individuals, and those with a history of disordered eating should consult with a healthcare professional before starting any new diet.

In general, it is important to listen to your body and make adjustments to the Mediterranean Refresh diet as needed to meet your individual needs and preferences. If you have any concerns or questions about whether the diet is suitable for you, it is recommended to consult with a healthcare professional

Chapter 1: Breakfast

Egg Toast with Vegetables (Healthy Breakfast Recipe)

Prep Time: 5 Minutes
Cook Time: 15 Minutes
Serves: 4

Ingredients:

- 4 to 5 large eggs
- Kosher salt
- ½ teaspoon sweet paprika
- ½ teaspoon red pepper flakes or 1 teaspoon Aleppo-style pepper
- 1 bell pepper, chopped
- ½ cup cherry tomatoes, halved or chopped
- 2 green onions, trimmed and chopped
- ¼ cup crumbled feta cheese
- 3 tablespoons chopped fresh parsley
- Extra virgin olive oil
- 4 slices of sandwich bread, thick cut

Directions:

1. Preheat the oven to 375°F and set a rack in the middle.
2. Beat and season the eggs. In a medium mixing bowl, add the eggs and season with kosher salt, paprika, and red pepper flakes or Aleppo-style pepper, and whisk.
3. Add the vegetables, etc. Add the chopped veggies, feta, and parsley, and a drizzle of good extra virgin olive oil.
4. Prepare the bread. Brush a sheet pan with olive oil and arrange the bread on it.
5. Top each slice of bread with a portion of the whisked egg mixture.
6. Bake. Place the sheet-pan on the middle rack of your heated oven. Bake for about 15 minutes or until the egg mixture is fully cooked and the veggies have softened a bit.

Nutritional Value (Amount per Serving):

Calories: 338; Fat: 26.37; Carb: 7.36; Protein: 18.55

Ultimate Falafel Sandwich

Prep Time: 50 Minutes
Cook Time: 10 Minutes
Serves: 6

Ingredients:

- 1 recipe Classic Falafel (or Baked Falafel)
- 6 Flatbreads or pita bread
- 1 recipe Quick Cucumber Sauce (or Tzatziki), Cilantro Sauce, or Tahini Sauce
- ½ cup hummus (optional)
- 2 medium tomatoes, chopped or 1 cup cherry tomatoes, halved
- 3 cups chopped romaine lettuce or green cabbage (or sliced cucumbers)
- 1/2 small red onion, sliced
- Chopped cilantro, flat leaf parsley, or dill, to garnish
- Optional: Storebought harissa, roasted eggplant for an over-the-top sandwich

Directions:

1. Make the falafel. (Note: The dried chickpeas must be soaked overnight.) Use the refrigeration time for the falafel dough to do the steps below.
2. If using homemade bread, make the flatbread (or make it in advance: it stores well!). If using store bought bread, warm the bread before serving in a 300 degree oven for a few minutes until pliable.
3. Make the sauce: either Quick Cucumber Sauce, Cilantro Sauce, or Tahini Sauce.
4. Chop the tomatoes, lettuce, and red onion.
5. Slather the bottom of the pita with hummus or some of the sauce, then add the falafel, chopped vegetables, and chopped herbs. Liberally spoon over the sauce.

Nutritional Value (Amount per Serving):

Calories: 137; Fat: 3.14; Carb: 23.97; Protein: 4.87

Easy Shakshuka Recipe

Prep Time: 10 Minutes
Cook Time: 30 Minutes
Serves: 6

Ingredients:

- Extra virgin olive oil
- 1 large yellow onion chopped
- 2 green peppers chopped
- 2 garlic cloves, chopped
- 1 teaspoon ground coriander
- 1 teaspoon sweet paprika
- ½ teaspoon ground cumin
- Pinch red pepper flakes optional
- Salt and pepper
- 6 medium tomatoes, chopped (about 6 cups chopped tomatoes)
- ½ cup tomato sauce
- 6 large eggs
- ¼ cup chopped fresh parsley leaves
- ¼ cup chopped fresh mint leaves

Directions:

1. Heat 3 tablespoon olive oil in a large cast iron skillet. Add the onions, green peppers, garlic, spices, pinch salt and pepper. Cook, stirring occasionally, until the vegetables have softened, about 5 minutes.
2. Add the tomatoes and tomato sauce. Cover and let simmer for about 15 minutes. Uncover and cook a bit longer to allow the mixture to reduce and thicken. Taste and adjust the seasoning to your liking.
3. Using a wooden spoon, make 6 indentations, or "wells," in the tomato mixture (make sure the indentations are spaced out). Gently crack an egg into each indention.
4. Reduce the heat, cover the skillet, and cook on low until the egg whites are set.
5. Uncover and add the fresh parsley and mint. You can add more black pepper or crushed red pepper, if you like. Serve with warm pita, challah, or crusty bread of your choice.

Nutritional Value (Amount per Serving):

Calories: 146; Fat: 7.59; Carb: 14.76; Protein: 5.37

Vegetarian Smashed Chickpea Toast

Prep Time: 3 Minutes
Cook Time: 6 Minutes
Serves: 4

Ingredients:

- 4 slices Tuscan country bread, about ½-inch in thickness (or similar hearty bread)
- Extra virgin olive oil to drizzle on bread
- 1 15-ounce can chickpeas, drained and rinsed
- 1 to 2 garlic cloves, minced
- 1 to 2 spring onions, white and green parts, trimmed and chopped
- 1 vine-ripened tomato, chopped
- Kosher salt, to taste
- 1 teaspoon ground cumin
- 1 teaspoon Aleppo pepper
- 2 hard-boiled eggs, peeled and sliced
- Fresh parsley for garnish

Directions:

1. Set a cast iron skillet or griddle over medium-high heat. Drizzle a little extra virgin olive oil over the bread slices. When the skillet is hot, arrange the bread in it (oiled side down).
2. Let the bread toast in the skillet for about a minute or until the bottom turns a nice golden-brown color. Drizzle a little more extra virgin olive oil on the top part of the bread and flip it over. Allow the bread to toast on the second side for about a minute or so. (You may need to toast the bread in batches, depending on the size of your skillet). Transfer the bread to a plate.
3. Remove it from the heat for about 2 minutes and allow it to cool slightly before adding the chickpeas (otherwise, the chickpeas will pop all over the place).
4. When the skillet is ready, return the skillet to a burner set over medium

heat. Add about 2 tablespoons extra virgin olive oil.

5. When the oil is shimmering, add the chickpeas, garlic, onions, and chopped tomato. Season with a good dash of kosher salt, the cumin, and Aleppo pepper. Cook, stirring occasionally until warmed through (about 3 to 5 minutes). Carefully taste and adjust seasoning to your liking.

6. Turn the heat off and, using the back of a fork or a potato masher, gently smash the chickpeas.

7. Top the toasted bread with the smashed chickpeas and add a slice or two of the hardboiled eggs on top. Finish with a little parsley and a drizzle of extra virgin olive oil. Enjoy warm or at room temperature.

Nutritional Value (Amount per Serving):

Calories: 288; Fat: 8.91; Carb: 38.36; Protein: 14.95

Sweet Potato Hash Recipe With Za'atar And Chickpeas

Prep Time: 10 Minutes
Cook Time: 20 Minutes
Serves: 1

Ingredients:

- 3 tablespoons extra-virgin olive oil
- 1 medium red onion, chopped
- 2 small sweet potatoes, about 1 ½ pounds total, peeled and cut into ½-inch cubes
- 1 cup canned chickpeas, drained and rinsed
- Kosher salt and ground black pepper
- 1 teaspoon ground coriander
- ½ teaspoon ground cumin
- ½ teaspoon sweet paprika
- ½ teaspoon ground turmeric
- 2 large garlic cloves, minced

- 1 large red bell pepper, cored, seeded and chopped
- 1 tablespoon za'atar, plus more as desired
- 1 teaspoon distilled white vinegar
- 4 large eggs

Directions:

1. In a 12-inch cast-iron skillet, heat the olive oil over medium-high heat until shimmering but not smoking. Add the red onion, sweet potatoes, and chickpeas. Season with a big pinch of salt and black pepper (about ½ teaspoon each). Add the coriander, cumin, paprika, and turmeric. Stir to combine. Cook, stirring frequently, until the onion is nicely caramelized and the sweet potatoes have softened quite a bit, 10 to 15 minutes.
2. Reduce the heat to medium. Add the garlic and bell pepper. Continue to cook, stirring frequently, until the pepper has softened and the potatoes are now cooked through, another 5 to 10 minutes. Sprinkle with the za'atar.
3. Meanwhile, bring a medium pot of water to a steady simmer over medium-low heat and add the vinegar. Break each egg into a small bowl or ramekin. Stir the simmering water gently and carefully slide each egg in; the egg whites should wrap around the yolk. Cook for 3 minutes exactly, then remove the eggs from the simmering water using a slotted spoon and put them on a paper towel to drain briefly. Season with a pinch of salt, pepper and a little more za'atar.
4. Divide the sweet potato hash among 4 bowls and top each with a poached egg. Serve immediately.

Nutritional Value (Amount per Serving):

Calories: 158; Fat: 4.24; Carb: 26; Protein: 4.77

Easy Oven Baked Eggs

Prep Time: 5 Minutes
Cook Time: 8 Minutes
Serves: 2

Ingredients:

- Extra virgin olive oil
- 2 to 4 Large eggs
- Kosher salt and black pepper
- Red pepper flakes or Aleppo pepper, optional
- ptional Toppings:
- Crumbled feta cheese
- Chopped chives
- Chopped parsley
- Microgreens
- Small diced tomatoes

Directions:

1. Prepare the oven: Preheat the oven to 375°F and position a rack in the middle.
2. Coat ramekins with oil: Brush the bottoms and sides of 2 to 4 small ramekins or oven-safe dishes with extra virgin olive oil.
3. Add egg(s): Crack 1 egg in each dish, depending on the size of the dish (a 4 ½ -inch round ramekin will take 2 eggs).
4. Bake: Arrange the ramekins on a sheet pan and place the sheet pan on the middle rack of the heated oven. Bake for about 8 minutes or until the egg whites are just set. The yolk should still be runny, so watch closely so you don't overcook them (remember, the egg whites will continue to set when you take them out of the oven). If you like the yolks to be on the firmer side, leave the eggs in the oven for a couple more minutes.
5. Garnish and serve: When the eggs are done to your liking, remove them from the oven and season with kosher salt, black pepper and, if you like a little heat, add a dash of red pepper flakes or Aleppo pepper. Garnish with the toppings of your choice (feta, fresh herbs, or small diced tomatoes). Serve immediately!

Nutritional Value (Amount per Serving):

Calories: 383; Fat: 27.92; Carb: 14.68; Protein: 20.46

Strata (Baked Egg Breakfast Casserole)

Prep Time: 20 Minutes
Cook Time: 1 Hour
Serves: 10

Ingredients:

- 2 teaspoons olive oil, plus more for greasing the baking dish
- 3 cups chopped spinach, packed
- 4 cloves garlic, minced
- 1 pound about 6 cups crusty bread, cut into large cubes
- 4 ounces chevre cheese
- 1 cup shredded parmesan cheese
- 3 large roasted red peppers, chopped (about 1 cup)
- 3 ounces prosciutto, torn to bite-size pieces
- 4 scallions or chives, chopped
- 8 eggs
- 3 cups whole milk
- 1 teaspoon Italian seasoning
- 1 teaspoon kosher salt
- ½ teaspoon black pepper

Directions:

1. Preheat the oven to 350°F. Grease a 9x13 baking dish with a little olive oil. Place it on a baking sheet.
2. In a large skillet set over medium heat, add 2 teaspoons of olive oil. When it shimmers add the garlic, saute until fragrant, about 1 minute. Add the spinach and stir until wilted and most of the moisture has evaporated. Remove from heat and turn off the burner.
3. Arrange the bread cubes in a single layer on the bottom of the pan. Layer on ⅓ of the cheeses, roasted red pepper, spinach, prosciutto, and scallions. Top with more bread and repeat the layering process until the ingredients are used up.

4. In a large bowl, whisk together the eggs, milk, italian seasoning, salt, and pepper. Pour it over the layered bread in the baking dish.
5. Transfer it to the oven to bake for 60 to 70 minutes or until a knife inserted in the center comes out clean and the strata is puffed up and slightly golden on the top.

Nutritional Value (Amount per Serving):

Calories: 419; Fat: 18.03; Carb: 45.13; Protein: 18.66

Challah French Toast With Orange Honey Glaze

Prep Time: 20 Minutes
Cook Time: 10 Minutes
Serves: 5

Ingredients:

- or The Orange Honey Syrup:
- ½ cup honey
- ¼ cup orange juice
- 2 oranges, zested and supremed
- or The French Toast:
- 1 loaf challah bread, about 8 to 10 thick slices
- 6 eggs
- 1 cup whole milk
- 1 ¾ teaspoon ground cinnamon
- 1 teaspoon almond extract
- ¼ teaspoon kosher salt
- 4 teaspoons granulated sugar
- 1 cup blueberries
- 4 tablespoons creme fraiche, optional

Directions:

1. Supreme the oranges: Zest each orange and set zest aside. Slice the top and bottom off of an orange so you have a flat surface to work with and the flesh of the orange is exposed. Starting at the top, move your knife downward slicing between the flesh of the orange and the white pith. Do this around the entire orange until there isn't any peel or pith attached.

2. Hold the orange over a small bowl to catch any juices, slowly cut each segment out from the membrane and place on a small plate. Repeat with the second orange. Once each orange has been segmented, squeeze the membranes to release any juices into the bowl.

3. Make the syrup: In a small saucepan set over medium low heat add ½ cup honey, and ¼ cup of orange juice from when you supremed the oranges. Heat, stirring occasionally just until the mixture is combined and pourable. Transfer to a small container.

4. Slice the bread: Slice the loaf into 1 or 1 ½ inch thick slices. You should end up with 8 to 10 slices depending upon the size of your loaf.

5. Make the custard: In a pie plate or wide shallow dish use a fork or whisk to combine the eggs, milk, ground cinnamon, almond extract, salt, sugar, and orange zest until well combined.

6. Soak the bread: Place as many slices as will fit in a single layer in the dish with the custard. Flip them over so both sides are coated.

7. Heat the skillet: Place 2 tablespoons of butter or ghee in a skillet set over medium heat. Once it sizzles add the soaked bread in a single layer. Cook on one side until golden brown, then flip and cook on the other side until golden brown.

8. Serve: Place two slices of french toast on a plate. Top with 1 tablespoon of creme fraiche, berries and orange slices. Drizzle with the orange honey syrup and serve. (If you have another orange laying around and you're feeling fancy, go ahead and zest a little over the top of the toast before serving.)

Nutritional Value (Amount per Serving):

Calories: 687; Fat: 21.47; Carb: 108.93; Protein: 17.79

Eggs Fra Diavolo (Eggs In Purgatory With A Twist)

Prep Time: 5 Minutes
Cook Time: 15 Minutes
Serves: 6

Ingredients:

- Extra virgin olive oil• 6 hardboiled eggs, peeled
- or The Spicy Tomato Sauce• 1 medium onion, yellow or red, chopped
- 5 garlic cloves, minced• 1 hot pepper such as jalapeño, chopped
- Kosher salt• 1 5 ounce can diced fire-roasted tomatoes
- ¼ cup tomato paste• 2 teaspoons dried oregano
- 1 to 2 teaspoon dried red pepper flakes or Aleppo pepper, more or less to your liking (if you like the sauce hot, you can add more)
- ½ cup basil or parsley, chopped

Directions:

1. In a 10-inch skillet or pan, heat about 2 tablespoons extra virgin olive oil over medium-high heat until shimmering. Carefully add the already boiled eggs and cook on all sides until the egg whites begin to crisp up and turn golden brown (use a splatter guard over your pan to keep the oil from splashing). Remove the eggs from the pan and set them on a plate or bowl for now.
2. In the same pan, add the onions, garlic, and jalapeno. Cook for 3 to 5 minutes, tossing regularly, until fragrant. Season with a big dash of kosher salt.
3. Add the diced tomatoes, tomato paste, and about ¼ cup of water. Season with another big dash of kosher salt. Add the oregano and red pepper flakes, if using. Bring the mixture to a boil, then lower the heat to medium-low and allow the tomatoes to simmer for about 10 minutes or so.
4. Add the eggs to the simmering tomato sauce and cook for another 3 minutes or until the eggs are warm.
5. Remove from the heat and finish with the parsley and a good drizzle of extra virgin olive oil. Serve with crusty bread or warmed flatbread.

Nutritional Value (Amount per Serving):

Calories: 120; Fat: 2g; Carb: 4g; Protein: 4g

Smoked Salmon Sandwich With Feta

Prep Time: 15 Minutes
Cook Time: 0 Minute
Serves: 4

Ingredients:

- 1 carrot, peeled and cut into thin, short sticks
- 3 radishes, cut into thin, short sticks
- 1 green onion, white and green parts, sliced into rounds
- Aleppo pepper (or red pepper flakes), to taste
- Kosher salt, to taste• 1 lime or lemon
- Extra virgin olive oil
- 1 small beet, peeled and cut into thin, short sticks
- 4 slices whole wheat bread, toasted
- 2 ounces quality feta cheese
- 5 to 6 ounces quality smoked salmon fillet

Directions:

1. In a small bowl, combine the carrots, radish, green onion, and beets. Season lightly with kosher salt and Aleppo pepper (or red pepper flakes). Add as good squeeze of the lime and a drizzle of extra virgin olive oil and toss.
2. Combine the feta cheese with a bit of olive oil and, using the back of your fork, break up the feta and mash it so it is easy to spread.
3. Spread some feta on each of the toasted bread slices. Add the smoked salmon on top and season with a pinch of red pepper flakes and a squeeze of lime, if you like. Add the veggies on top and serve!

Nutritional Value (Amount per Serving):

Calories: 374; Fat: 9.16; Carb: 59.37; Protein: 18.12

Chapter 2: Lunch

Shrimp Lettuce Wraps Recipe

Prep Time: 6 Minutes
Cook Time: 3 Minutes
Serves: 4

Ingredients:

- 1 Tahini Green Goddess Dressing recipe
- 1 Persian Cucumber or ¼ English cucumber, halved lengthwise and thinly sliced into half moons
- ½ cup cherry tomatoes, halved
- 2 baby bell peppers, sliced into rings
- 1 to 2 green onions, trimmed, whites and greens chopped
- ½ cup Basil leaves, cilantro, or parsley
- 8 to 10 ounces large shrimp, peeled and deveined
- Kosher salt
- ½ teaspoon garlic powder
- ½ teaspoon dried oregano
- Extra virgin olive oil
- ½ lemon
- 1 head butter lettuce or other artisan lettuce you like

Directions:

1. Make the tahini green goddess dressing according to this recipe.
2. Prepare and slice the vegetables and set them aside.
3. Pat the shrimp dry and toss it with kosher salt, the garlic powder, and dried oregano.
4. Heat 1 tablespoon extra virgin olive oil in a large non-stick pan. Add the shrimp and cook for 2 to 3 minutes or until just pink and no longer grey. Immediately squeeze the lemon all over the shrimp.
5. Assemble the lettuce wrap. Take one lettuce leaf (or you can overlap two leaves if you're using smaller lettuce leaves) and arrange some of the veggies and fresh herbs on top. Add 1 to 2 shrimp. And finish with a drizzle of the green goddess dressing.
6. Serve the lettuce wraps with a bit more of the green goddess dressing on the side.

Nutritional Value (Amount per Serving):

Calories: 237; Fat: 16.47; Carb: 11; Protein: 11.83

Savory Mushroom And Leeks Galette

Prep Time: 15 Minutes
Cook Time: 25 Minutes
Serves: 8

Ingredients:

- 4 tablespoons extra virgin olive oil
- 1 large leek (or two medium leeks, white parts only, finely chopped, about 3 cups)
- Kosher salt and black pepper
- ½ teaspoon dried red pepper flakes
- 1 pound mushrooms (any kind, stemmed, cleaned, and roughly chopped, about 7 cups)
- 3 fresh thyme sprigs, leaves only
- ⅓cup frozen peas
- 9-inch pie dough round (store bought is fine)
- 1 tablespoon nutritional yeast
- 1 large egg (whisked)
- flaky sea salt for sprinklin

Directions:

1. Preheat the oven to 425 degrees F. Line a sheet pan with parchment paper
2. In a large skillet over medium heat, combine 3 tablespoon of olive oil, the leeks, salt, pepper, and red pepper flakes. Cook, stirring occasionally, until the leeks are soft, about 4 minutes.
3. Push the leeks to the perimeter of the pan, then add the remaining 1 tablespoon olive oil and the mushrooms. Cook until the mushrooms have given off their juices and then shriveled, about 10 minutes, leaving the leeks on the perimeter.
4. Stir in the thyme and peas and cook another minute, folding in the leeks.
5. Place the pie dough on the prepared sheet pan and sprinkle the nutritional yeast all over it, pressing the flakes into the dough with your fingers or a rolling pin

6. Spoon the mushroom-leek filling into the center, spreading it in an even layer and leaving a 1-inch border, then folding the edges over the filling, overlapping aa sou work your way around the perimeter.
7. Brush the dough with the whisked egg and sprinkle with the sea salt.
8. Bake in the heated oven until the crust is golden, 20 to 25 minutes

Nutritional Value (Amount per Serving):

Calories: 1360; Fat: 68.39; Carb: 179.74; Protein: 15.18

Mediterranean Grilled Eggplant With Whipped Feta

Prep Time: 30 Minutes
Cook Time: 10 Minutes
Serves: 6

Ingredients:

- 1 globe eggplant, sliced into ½-inch rounds
- Kosher salt
- extra virgin olive oil
- live Oil, Garlic, And Jalapeno Sauce
- extra virgin olive oil
- 2 garlic cloves, minced
- 1 lemon, juice of
- 1 jalapeno, finely chopped, remove ribs and seeds if you need it to be more mild
- 1 to 2 teaspoons sumac
- o Serve (Optional)
- whipped feta (make this recipe), optional

Directions:

1. Slice and salt the eggplant. Lay the eggplant slices on a large tray lined with paper towel. Salt the eggplant generously and let it sit for 20 to 30 minutes while you work on other things. Beads of water will form. Wipe the

eggplant dry and remove excess salt before grilling.

2. Make the garlic, jalapeno and olive oil sauce. In a small bowl, combine 3 tablespoons olive oil with the lemon juice, garlic, and jalapeno. Add a pinch of kosher salt and set aside (the lemon and olive oil will tame the hot peppers and the pungent taste of garlic).

3. If serving with whipped feta, follow this recipe but you do not need the nuts in this case.

4. When ready, heat a gas grill or an indoor griddle over medium-high and lightly oil the grates. Make sure the grill is fully heated before adding the eggplant.

5. Brush the eggplant slices on one side with olive oil.

6. Arrange the eggplant on the heated grill, oiled side down first. Grill anywhere for 3 to 4 minutes on this side or until some char marks form on the bottom, then turn over and brush the other side of the eggplant with olive oil. Cook for another 3 to 4 minutes or until the eggplant is tender and good char marks have formed on both sides.

7. Arrange the grilled eggplant on a large platter and immediately season with sumac and drizzle the olive oil and jalapeno mixture all over. Add the plate of feta and warmed pita bread for serving.

Nutritional Value (Amount per Serving):

Calories: 195; Fat: 10.7; Carb: 11.53; Protein: 14.48

Cauliflower Fritters Recipe WithCumin And Mint Yogurt

Prep Time: 15 Minutes
Cook Time: 5 Minutes
Serves: 16

Ingredients:

- or The Mint Yogurt
- ½ teaspoon dried mint
- 1 cup Greek yogurt
- 2 tablespoon lemon juice

- 1 tablespoon olive oil
- ½ teaspoon salt
- or The Cauliflower Fritters
- 1 small cauliflower, cut into 1 ½-inch florets (3 cups florets)
- 1 cup all-purpose flour
- 1 cup fresh parsley, finely chopped
- 1 small onion, finely chopped (about ¾ cup)
- 2 eggs
- 1 ½ teaspoon cumin
- ¾ teaspoon ground cinnamon
- ½ teaspoon turmeric
- ½ teaspoon Aleppo pepper, (or ¼ teaspoon red pepper flakes)
- ½ teaspoon baking powder
- Kosher salt and black pepper
- 1 cup sunflower oil

Directions:

1. To make the yogurt, place all the ingredients for the mint yogurt in a bowl. Mix to combine and keep in the fridge until ready to serve.
2. Bring a medium saucepan of salted water to a boil and add the cauliflower. Simmer for 4 minutes, then (making sure to reserve 3 to 4 tablespoons of the cooking water) drain into a colander.
3. Using a fork or a potato masher, crush the cauliflower, then transfer it to a large bowl.
4. Add the flour, parsley, onion, eggs, cumin, cinnamon, turmeric, Aleppo pepper flakes, baking powder, and 1 ¼ salt and a good grind of black pepper. Add 3 tablespoons of the cooking water and mix well to combine.
5. Line a large plate with paper towels.
6. In a large saute pan (about 9 inches wide), heat the oil. Once the oil is hot, carefully spoon 2 to 3 tablespoons of batter per fritter into the oil. You'll need to do this in batches (adding 4 to 5 fritters at a time) so as not to crowd the pan, and use a spatula to keep them apart. Fry for about 4 to 5 minutes, flipping over halfway through, until both sides are golden brown (mine took 2 minutes on each side).
7. Using a slotted spoon, transfer the cooked fritters to the prepared plate and set aside while you continue with the remaining batches.
8. Serve warm or at room temperature, with the mint yogurt on the side.

Nutritional Value (Amount per Serving):

Calories: 193; Fat: 16.39; Carb: 9.14; Protein: 3.08

Spanish Paella Recipe

Prep Time: 15 Minutes
Cook Time: 30 Minutes
Serves: 4

Ingredients:

- 1 medium yellow onion
- 6 garlic cloves
- 2 to 3 roma or plum tomatoes (1 1/2 cups finely chopped)
- 1/4 cup olive oil, divided
- 1/2 pound shrimp, peel and deveined
- 1 1/2 teaspoons smoked paprika, divided
- 1/4 teaspoon red pepper flakes
- 1 large pinch saffron
- 1 1/2 teaspoons kosher salt, divided
- 3 cups seafood stock or vegetable stock
- 1 1/2 cups short grain Bomba rice or arborio rice
- 1/4 cup frozen peas, thawed under water
- 1/2 cup artichoke hearts, quartered
- 1 to 2 roasted red bell peppers, cut into strips
- Lemon wedges from 1/2 lemon
- Chopped parsley, for garnish

Directions:

1. Prep the vegetables: Mince the onion. Mince the garlic. Finely chop the tomatoes, removing the cores but keeping the seeds with their juices.
2. Measure out the ingredients: Measure out all the remaining ingredients before you start. The cooking process goes fast!
3. Cook the shrimp: Dry the shrimp and add it to a bowl with 1/2 teaspoon smoked paprika and 1/4 teaspoon kosher salt. In your largest skillet or a 4-serving paella pan, heat 1 tablespoon olive oil over medium heat. Add the shrimp and saute until it is just barely opaque, about 1 to 2 minutes per

side. Remove the shrimp and set it aside.

4. Cook the paella: In the same pan, heat 3 tablespoons olive oil on medium heat. Saute the onion and garlic until just translucent, about 3 minutes, stirring frequently. Add the chopped tomatoes, the remaining 1 teaspoon smoked paprika and red pepper flakes, and cook until the tomatoes have broken down and most of the liquid is evaporated, about 5 minutes. Stir in the stock, saffron and 1 1/4 teaspoon kosher salt. Sprinkle the rice evenly across the broth and tap the pan with a spoon to evenly spread the rice. Bring to a medium simmer and cook without stirring until liquid is absorbed, about 18 to 22 minutes (adjust the cook time as necessary if using a skillet).

5. Adjust the heat as necessary: If your pan is large enough to span multiple burners on your stovetop, adjust the heat on each burner so you achieve a steady medium simmer. Rotate the pan every few minutes for an even cook.

6. Add the artichoke, peas and roasted red pepper: When the top of the rice is beginning to show through the liquid (about 10 minutes into the cook time), press the artichokes and peas lightly into the rice. Add the strips of red pepper over the top.

7. Assess whether the paella is done: In last few minutes, carefully watch the paella and rotate pan more frequently. As the paella finishes, you'll see the steam start to slow down as the water cooks out. If desired, peek at the bottom of a pan by using a knife to scrape back the rice — you shouldn't see any standing water. The sound will start to change from a simmer to a crackle. This indicates the crust is forming. Let the crackling continue for about 2 minutes before removing from the heat. If you smell any burning, remove immediately.

8. Add the shrimp and serve: When the paella is done, add the shrimp to top of paella and squeeze the lemon wedges onto the top of the pan. Sprinkle with a pinch or two of kosher salt and add the parsley, if using. Serve with additional lemon wedges.

Nutritional Value (Amount per Serving):

Calories: 319; Fat: 8g; Carb: 43g; Protein: 17g

Pasta e Ceci (Italian Chickpea Soup)

Prep Time: 5 Minutes
Cook Time: 25 Minutes
Serves: 4

Ingredients:

- Cooking spray
- 2 pounds gold potatoes, halved and sliced
- 1 yellow onion, cut into medium wedges
- 10 ounces canned vegan potato cream soup
- 8 ounces coconut milk   • 1 cup tofu, crumbled
- 1/2 cup veggie stock
- Salt and black pepper to the taste
- 1 tablespoons parsley, chopped

Directions:

1. Peel and small dice the onion. Mince the garlic. Chop the kale into bite-sized pieces.
2. In a large pot or Dutch oven, heat the olive oil over medium high heat. Add the onion and saute for 5 to 6 minutes until the onions are just translucent. Add the garlic and tomato paste and saute for 1 minute.
3. Add the vegetable broth, tomatoes and juices, chopped basil, drained and rinsed chickpeas, oregano, thyme, red pepper flakes, Parmesan rind (or grated Parmesan) and kosher salt. Bring it to a simmer, then cook 10 minutes on medium low.
4. Add the pasta and kale and cook until pasta is just al dente, about 8 to 10 minutes.
5. Taste and add fresh ground black pepper and more kosher salt to taste. Remove the Parmesan rind. If desired, garnish with torn basil leaves and Parmesan cheese shavings. The soup will continue to thicken as it cools.

Nutritional Value (Amount per Serving):

Calories: 337; Fat: 10.95; Carb: 50.21; Protein: 14.12g

Simple Red Lentil Soup

Prep Time: 10 Minutes
Cook Time: 15 Minutes
Serves: 6

Ingredients:

- 3 large carrots
- 1 medium yellow onion
- 3 celery ribs
- 6 garlic cloves
- ¼ cup olive oil
- 2 quarts vegetable broth
- 1 cup water
- 1 pound split red lentils
- 1 ½ tablespoons smoked paprika
- 1 ½ teaspoons lemon zest
- 1 teaspoon kosher salt
- Fresh ground black pepper
- Greek yogurt or sour cream (or cashew cream for vegan), for serving
- Cilantro, for serving

Directions:

1. Peel the carrots. Finely dice the carrot, onion, and celery. Mince the garlic.
2. In a large pot or Dutch oven, heat the olive oil over medium heat. Add the onion, carrots and celery, and sauté until the carrots are tender, about 5 to 7 minutes.
3. Stir in the garlic and sauté for 1 minute. Add the broth, water, red lentils, smoked paprika, lemon zest, kosher salt and fresh ground pepper.
4. Bring to a low simmer, then cover halfway and gently simmer until the lentils are just soft but before they start to break apart, about 7 to 10

minutes. Watch closely and taste to assess doneness. The finished soup should be brothy with the lentils just soft; cooking past this point yields a very thick stew which is just as delicious but less soup-like. (If you'd like, you can add handfuls of greens in the last few minutes, like chopped spinach or kale).

5. Taste and add additional salt to taste, and a few grinds black pepper. Leftovers can become very thick, so you can add a little water or broth when reheating.

Nutritional Value (Amount per Serving):

Calories: 465; Fat: 16.5; Carb: 60.39; Protein: 22.18

Easy Shakshuka with Feta

Prep Time: 10 Minutes
Cook Time: 25 Minutes
Serves: 4

Ingredients:

- 1 teaspoon coriander seeds
- 1 teaspoon cumin seeds
- 1 teaspoon fennel seeds
- 2 tablespoons olive oil
- 1 red bell pepper
- 1 large yellow onion
- 1 teaspoon smoked paprika
- 1 teaspoon kosher salt, plus more for sprinkling
- 1 28 ounce can diced tomatoes
- 1 15 ounce can white beans, drained and rinsed
- 4 to 6 large eggs, to your preference
- Freshly ground black pepper
- ½ cup fresh parsley or cilantro leaves
- ½ cup feta cheese crumbles

Directions:

1. Thinly slice the pepper. Thinly slice the onion.
2. Set a dry skillet, preferably cast iron, over medium heat. Add the coriander, cumin, and fennel seeds, then toast until fragrant, about 2 minutes. Carefully transfer the seeds to a plate to cool, then grind in a mortar and pestle or spice grinder.
3. Heat the olive oil in the same skillet over medium-high heat. Add the bell pepper and onion in an even layer, then do not be tempted to stir or fuss with them. Let them get a good, dark char, 3 to 4 minutes, before giving a quick stir and cooking a bit more until nearly all of the pepper and onion are blackened in parts. This process will take about 10 minutes.
4. Add the ground spices, paprika, and kosher salt. Stir for 1 minute before carefully tipping in the tomatoes. Let this mixture come to a simmer before stirring in the white beans. Bring everything to a gently boil, then lower the heat to a steady simmer. Simmer for 5 minutes, or until the tomatoes have thickened.
5. Carve out a little divot for each of the eggs you plan to cook, then carefully crack them in. Add a bit of kosher salt and black pepper to each egg then cover the skillet with a lid (or sheet pan if you can't find a matching lid). Cook over low heat until the eggs are just set, 4 to 6 minutes.
6. Chop the cilantro. Finish by garnishing with the fresh herbs and feta. Serve immediately.

Nutritional Value (Amount per Serving):

Calories: 549; Fat: 38.8; Carb: 18.35; Protein: 33.48

Lentil Salad with Feta

Prep Time: 15 Minutes
Cook Time: 15 Minutes
Serves: 8–10

Ingredients:

- For the lentils
- 1 pound black beluga lentils or French lentils

- 1 quart vegetable broth+ 2 cups water
- 1 teaspoon kosher salt
- 1 teaspoon dried thyme
- ½ teaspoon garlic powder
- For the lentil salad
- 2 tablespoons red wine vinegar
- 2 tablespoons lemon juice + zest of 1 lemon
- ½ teaspoon kosher salt + fresh ground pepper
- 1 cup baby arugula, plus more to serve
- 1 cup feta cheese crumbles, plus more for garnish
- ½ cup pistachios, plus more for garnish
- 3 radishes, for garnish

Directions:

1. For the lentils: In a large saucepan or deep skillet, simmer the lentils with the broth, water, kosher salt, thyme, and garlic powder for about 15 to 20 minutes until tender. Drain excess liquid.
2. Make the dressing: In a large bowl, whisk together the red wine vinegar, lemon juice, lemon zest, Dijon mustard, onion powder, and oregano. Whisk in the olive oil 1 tablespoon at a time until it's creamy and emulsified.
3. Chop the veggies: Thinly slice the shallot. Thinly slice the red pepper, then cut the slices in half to make pieces about 2-inches long. If using the herbs, chop them.

lemon juice, lemon zest, Dijon mustard, onion powder, and oregano. Whisk in the olive oil 1 tablespoon at a time until it's creamy and emulsified.
3. Chop the veggies: Thinly slice the shallot. Thinly slice the red pepper, then cut the slices in half to make pieces about 2-inches long. If using the herbs, chop them.
4. Mix together the salad: Place the lentils in the large bowl with the dressing. Add the shallot, pepper, herbs, baby arugula, feta cheese, and pistachios. Add the ½ teaspoon kosher salt and fresh ground pepper and mix to combine.
5. Serve: If desired, serve over arugula. Garnish with thinly sliced radish, with an additional sprinkle of feta and pistachios. Refrigerate any leftovers for up to 4 days (if you're planning to make for lunches, omit the pistachios). It saves well and leftovers taste even better!

Nutritional Value (Amount per Serving):

Calories: 254; Fat: 16.35; Carb: 21.86; Protein: 9.64

Italian Lentil Soup

Prep Time: 10 Minutes
Cook Time: 30 Minutes
Serves: 4 To 6

Ingredients:

- 1 large yellow onion
- 3 garlic cloves
- 1 15-ounce can quartered artichoke hearts
- ½ bunch Tuscan kale (also labeled as Lacinato, dinosaur kale or cavolo nero)
- 2 tablespoons olive oil
- 1 tablespoon dried oregano
- 1 tablespoon dried basil
- 1 cup dried red lentils
- 2 cups water
- 1 bay leaf
- ¼ teaspoon red pepper flakes
- 1 teaspoon kosher salt
- 2 28-ounce cans fire roasted whole tomatoes
- Shaved Parmesan cheese (optional), for garnish

Directions:

1. Dice the onion. Mince the garlic. Drain the artichoke hearts, and chop them into bite sized pieces. Wash and thinly slice the kale into ribbons.
2. In a large soup pot, heat the olive oil over medium heat and saute the onion for 5 minutes, until translucent. Add the minced garlic, dried oregano, and dried basil. Saute for another minute.
3. Add the red lentils, water, red pepper flakes, kosher salt, and 1 bay leaf and bring to a boil.
4. Once boiling, reduce to a simmer and add the kale, artichokes, and the liquid from the whole tomatoes. Then chop the whole tomatoes into bite

sized pieces, and add them to the pot.

5. Simmer for 20 minutes, until the lentils are tender. Be careful not to overcook the lentils, or they will become too soft.

6. Taste, and additional kosher salt as necessary. Serve with a drizzle of olive oil and shaved Parmesan cheese.

Nutritional Value (Amount per Serving):

Calories: 581; Fat: 16.93; Carb: 90.23; Protein: 23.59

Skillet Chicken with Olives

Prep Time: 10 Minutes
Cook Time: 10 Minutes
Serves: 4

Ingredients:

- 4 boneless skinless chicken thighs (about 1 pound)
- 1 teaspoon dried rosemary, crushed
- 1/2 teaspoon pepper
- 1/4 teaspoon salt
- 1 tablespoon olive oil
- 1/2 cup pimiento-stuffed olives, coarsely chopped
- 1/4 cup white wine or chicken broth
- 1 tablespoon drained capers, optional

Directions:

1. Sprinkle chicken with rosemary, pepper and salt. In a large skillet, heat oil over medium-high heat. Brown chicken on both sides.

2. Add olives, wine and, if desired, capers. Reduce heat; simmer, covered, 2-3 minutes or until a thermometer inserted in chicken reads 170°F.

Nutritional Value (Amount per Serving):

Calories: 336; Fat: 11.43; Carb: 1.79; Protein: 53.51

Mediterranean Pork And Orzo

Prep Time: 10 Minutes
Cook Time: 20 Minutes
Serves: 6

Ingredients:

- 1-1/2 pounds pork tenderloin
- 1 teaspoon coarsely ground pepper
- 2 tablespoons olive oil
- 3 quarts water
- 1-1/4 cups uncooked orzo pasta
- 1/4 teaspoon salt
- 1 package (6 ounces) fresh baby spinach
- 1 cup grape tomatoes, halved
- 3/4 cup crumbled feta cheese

Directions:

1. Rub pork with pepper; cut into 1-in. cubes. In a large nonstick skillet, heat oil over medium heat. Add pork; cook and stir until no longer pink, 8-10 minutes.
2. Meanwhile, in a Dutch oven, bring water to a boil. Stir in orzo and salt; cook, uncovered, 8 minutes. Stir in spinach; cook until orzo is tender and spinach is wilted, 45-60 seconds longer. Drain.
3. Add tomatoes to pork; heat through. Stir in orzo mixture and cheese.

Nutritional Value (Amount per Serving):

Calories: 249; Fat: 13.23; Carb: 11.14; Protein: 21.89

Mediterranean Chickpeas

Prep Time: 10 Minutes
Cook Time: 15 Minutes
Serves: 4

Ingredients:

- 1 cup water
- 3/4 cup uncooked whole wheat couscous
- 1 tablespoon olive oil
- 1 medium onion, chopped
- 2 garlic cloves, minced
- 1 can (15 ounces) chickpeas or garbanzo beans, rinsed and drained
- 1 can (14-1/2 ounces) no-salt-added stewed tomatoes, cut up
- 1 can (14 ounces) water-packed artichoke hearts, rinsed, drained and chopped
- 1/2 cup pitted Greek olives, coarsely chopped
- 1 tablespoon lemon juice
- 1/2 teaspoon dried oregano
- Dash pepper
- Dash cayenne pepper

Directions:

1. In a small saucepan, bring water to a boil. Stir in couscous. Remove from heat; let stand, covered, 5-10 minutes or until water is absorbed. Fluff with a fork.
2. Meanwhile, in a large nonstick skillet, heat oil over medium-high heat. Add onion; cook and stir until tender. Add garlic; cook 1 minute longer. Sir in remaining ingredients; heat through, stirring occasionally. Serve with couscous.

Nutritional Value (Amount per Serving):

Calories: 277; Fat: 7.97; Carb: 47.05; Protein: 9

Mediterranean Chicken Stir-Fry

Prep Time: 10 Minutes
Cook Time: 20 Minutes
Serves: 4

Ingredients:

- 2 cups water
- 1 cup quick-cooking barley
- 1 pound boneless skinless chicken breasts, cubed
- 3 teaspoons olive oil, divided
- 1 medium onion, chopped
- 2 medium zucchini, chopped
- 2 garlic cloves, minced
- 1 teaspoon dried oregano
- 1/2 teaspoon dried basil
- 1/4 teaspoon salt
- 1/4 teaspoon pepper
- Dash crushed red pepper flakes
- 2 plum tomatoes, chopped
- 1/2 cup pitted Greek olives, chopped
- 1 tablespoon minced fresh parsley

Directions:

1. In a small saucepan, bring water to a boil. Stir in barley. Reduce heat; cover and simmer for 10-12 minutes or until barley is tender. Remove from the heat; let stand for 5 minutes.
2. Meanwhile, in a large skillet or wok, stir-fry chicken in 2 teaspoons oil until no longer pink. Remove and keep warm.
3. Stir-fry onion in remaining oil for 3 minutes. Add the zucchini, garlic, oregano, basil, salt, pepper and pepper flakes; stir-fry 2-4 minutes longer or until vegetables are crisp-tender. Add the chicken, tomatoes, olives and parsley. Serve with barley.

Nutritional Value (Amount per Serving):

Calories: 275; Fat: 8.44; Carb: 22.32; Protein: 27.53

Baked Cod Recipe With Lemon And Garlic

Prep Time: 10 Minutes
Cook Time: 12 Minutes
Serves: 5

Ingredients:

- 1.5 lb Cod fillet pieces, 4-6 pieces
- ¼ cup chopped fresh parsley leaves
- 5 tablespoon fresh lemon juice
- 2 tablespoon melted butter
- or Coating
- 1 teaspoon ground coriander
- ¾ teaspoon sweet Spanish paprika
- ¾ teaspoon ground cumin
- ¾ teaspoon salt
- ½ teaspoon black pepper

- emon Sauce
- 5 tbsp extra virgin olive oil
- 5 garlic cloves, minced
- ⅓cup all-purpose flour

Directions:

1. Preheat oven to 400 degrees F.
2. Mix together the lemon juice, olive oil, and melted butter in a shallow bowl (do not add the garlic yet). Set aside.
3. In another shallow bowl, mix the all-purpose flour, spices, salt and pepper. Set next to the lemon sauce.
4. Pat the fish dry. Dip the fish in the lemon sauce then dip it in the flour mixture. Shake off excess flour. Reserve the lemon sauce for later.
5. Heat 2 tablespoon olive oil in a cast iron skillet (or an oven-safe pan) over medium-high heat (watch the oil to be sure it is shimmering but not smoking). Add the fish and sear on each side to give it some color, but do not fully cook (about 2 minutes on each side). Remove the skillet from heat.
6. To the remaining lemon sauce, add the minced garlic and mix. Drizzle all over the fish fillets.
7. Bake in the heated oven until the fish flakes easily with a fork (10 minutes

should do it, but begin checking earlier). Remove from the heat and sprinkle chopped parsley. Serve immediately.

Nutritional Value (Amount per Serving):

Calories: 232; Fat: 11.45; Carb: 9.3; Protein: 22.26

Quick Oven Roasted Tomatoes Recipe

Cook Time: 30 Minutes
Serves: 6

Ingredients:

- 2 lb Smaller Tomatoes, halved (I used Campari tomatoes)
- 2 to 3 garlic cloves, minced   • Kosher salt and black pepper
- 2 teaspoon fresh thyme, stems removed   • 1 teaspoon sumac
- ½ teaspoon dry chili pepper flakes, I used Aleppo Pepper which is milder
- Extra virgin olive oil, I used Private Reserve Greek extra virgin olive oil
- Crumbled feta cheese, optional

Directions:

1. Preheat the oven to 450 degrees F.
2. Place the tomato halves in a large mixing bowl. Add minced garlic, salt, pepper, fresh thyme, and spices. Drizzle a generous amount, about ¼ cup or more, quality extra virgin olive. Toss to coat.
3. Transfer the tomatoes to a baking sheet with a rim. Spread the tomatoes in one single layer, flesh side up.
4. Roast in your heated oven for 30 to 35 minutes or until the tomatoes have collapsed to your desired doneness.
5. Remove from heat. If you are planning to serve it soon, feel free to garnish with more fresh thyme and a few sprinkles of feta cheese. Enjoy warm or at room temperature.

Nutritional Value (Amount per Serving):

Calories: 96; Fat: 5.74; Carb: 7.03; Protein: 5.54

Crustless Zucchini Quiche Recipe

Prep Time: 15 Minutes
Cook Time: 30 Minutes
Serves: 8

Ingredients:

- 1 medium tomato sliced into thin rounds
- Private Reserve extra virgin olive oil
- 1 zucchini, sliced into rounds (about 8 ounces sliced zucchini)
- 3 shallots, sliced into rounds (about 3.5 ounces sliced shallots)
- Kosher salt and pepper
- 1 tsp sweet Spanish paprika, divided
- 1/2 cup part-skim shredded mozzarella (nearly 2 ounces)
- 2 tbsp grated Parmesan (about 0.35 ounces)
- 3 large eggs, beaten
- 2/3 cup skim milk
- 1/4 tsp baking powder
- 1/2 cup white whole wheat flour OR all-purpose flour (about 2 ounces), sifted
- 1/4 cup packed fresh parsley (about 0.2 ounces)

Directions:

1. Preheat the oven to 350 degrees F.
2. Arrange sliced tomatoes on paper towel and sprinkle with salt. Leave for a few minutes, then pat dry.
3. Meanwhile, in a large cooking skillet, heat 2 tbsp Private Reserve extra virgin olive oil over medium heat until shimmering but not smoking. Add zucchini and shallots. Season with kosher salt, pepper, and 1/2 tsp sweet paprika. Raise heat slightly, and sautee, tossing regularly, until vegetables

are tender and nicely colored (with some brown spots on zucchini).

4. Transfer the cooked zucchini and shallots mixture to the bottom of a lightly oiled 9-inch pie dish like this one. Arrange sliced tomatoes on top. Add mozzarella, and Parmesan (spread evenly across).

5. In a mixing bowl, whisk together eggs, milk, remaining 1/2 tsp paprika, baking powder, flour, and fresh parsley.

6. Pour egg mixture into the pie dish on top of the cheese mixture.

7. Bake in 350 degrees F heated-oven for about 30 minutes or until the egg mixture is well set in the dish. Remove from oven and wait 5 to 7 minutes before slicing to serve (Quiche will puff up slightly because of the baking powder, but will quickly go down as it sits.)

Nutritional Value (Amount per Serving):

Calories: 86; Fat: 2.93; Carb: 11.24; Protein: 3.84

10-Minute Garlic Parmesan Shrimp Recipe

Prep Time: 5 Minutes
Cook Time: 5 Minutes
Serves: 6

Ingredients:

- 1 pound jumbo shrimp, peeled and deveined
- Kosher salt and black pepper
- red pepper flakes, to taste
- 4 large garlic cloves, crushed or minced
- ½ cup chopped parsley, optional
- 1 lemon, zested and juiced
- Extra virgin olive oil
- 1 teaspoon oregano
- ¼ cup grated parmesan, more to your liking

Directions:

1. Pat the shrimp dry and season with a big pinch of kosher salt, black pepper and red pepper flakes. Drizzle with extra virgin olive oil and toss to be sure the shrimp is well-coated with the oil.
2. In a large bowl, combine garlic, parsley (if using), lemon juice and zest, ¼ cup extra virgin olive oil, oregano, and red pepper flakes. Season lightly with salt and pepper. Whisk together.
3. Heat a grill or indoor griddle to medium-high and lightly oil the grates. Grill the shrimp on each side until just pink (about 5 minutes or so in total, depending on the size of the shrimp).
4. Immediately remove the shrimp from the heat and toss it in the prepared olive oil and garlic mixture. Add the parmesan cheese, then toss to coat.
5. Transfer to a serving plate and serve immediately.

Nutritional Value (Amount per Serving):

Calories: 110; Fat: 2.32; Carb: 4.35; Protein: 17.39

Chapter 3: Dinner

Feta Garbanzo Bean Salad

Prep Time: 10 Minutes
Cook Time: 5 Minutes
Serves: 4

Ingredients:

- 1 can (15 ounces) garbanzo beans or chickpeas, rinsed and drained
- 1-1/2 cups coarsely chopped English cucumber (about 1/2 medium)
- 1 can (2-1/4 ounces) sliced ripe olives, drained
- 1 medium tomato, seeded and chopped
- 1/4 cup thinly sliced red onion
- 1/4 cup chopped fresh parsley
- 3 tablespoons olive oil
- 1 tablespoon lemon juice
- 1/4 teaspoon salt
- 1/8 teaspoon pepper
- 5 cups torn mixed salad greens
- 1/2 cup crumbled feta cheese

Directions:

1. Place the first 11 ingredients in a large bowl; toss to combine. Sprinkle with cheese.

Nutritional Value (Amount per Serving):

Calories: 330; Fat: 25.18; Carb: 18.74; Protein: 8.62

Mediterranean Falafel Bowls

Prep Time: 30 Minutes
Cook Time: 0 Minute
Serves: 4

Ingredients:

- Hummus, homemade or store bought
- Tabouli or Salad of Choice, use this homemade tabouli salad recipe
- 16 Falafels, prepared ahead from this authentic falafel recipe or air-fryer falafel recipe, or store-bought from your favorite Middle Eastern restaurant
- 2 Medium Vine-Ripe Tomatoes, halved and sliced
- 1 English Cucumber, halved and sliced
- 6 Radishes, halved and sliced
- 1/2 Medium Red Onion, thinly sliced
- 4 ounces Feta Cheese, sliced
- Extra virgin olive oil, for drizzling, try our rich and peppery Early Harvest or Spanish Hojiblanca EVOO
- Sumac, optional for seasoning

Directions:

1. Using shallow dinner bowls, start by spreading about 3 to 4 tablespoons of hummus on one side. Next, add the salad, then add 3 to 4 falafel patties.
2. Fill the empty spots in your bowls with the fresh vegetables, olive and pickles, and sliced feta cheese.
3. Finish each bowl with a generous drizzle of extra virgin olive oil and a dash of sumac to season (optional).

Nutritional Value (Amount per Serving):

Calories: 371; Fat: 24.46; Carb: 25.32; Protein: 13.49

Pan Seared Scallops

Prep Time: 10 Minutes
Cook Time: 5 Minutes
Serves: 4

Ingredients:

- 1 pound sea scallops, thawed if frozen
- Kosher salt
- 2 tablespoons neutral oil
- 1 tablespoon salted butter
- Lemon wedges, for serving

Directions:

1. Thaw the scallops, if frozen (see above).
2. Brine the scallops: In a shallow dish, mix together 4 cups room temperature water and 2 tablespoons kosher salt. Place the scallops in the water and wait for 10 minutes.
3. Remove the scallops and dry thoroughly. Lightly season with a several pinches kosher salt.
4. Heat the oil in a large skillet over high heat. If using a medium skillet, cook the scallops in two batches. Once the oil is hot, add the scallops and cook without turning for 2 to 3 minutes, until an even brown crust clearly forms on bottom.
5. Flip scallops with tongs. Cook additional 2 to 3 minutes on the other side, until a crust just forms on bottom and the center of the scallop is almost opaque.
6. Turn off the heat and add the butter. When it melts, spoon the melted butter over the scallops and serve with a squeeze of lemon. Or, go to Lemon Herb Scallop Sauce to make a 2 minute pan sauce.

Nutritional Value (Amount per Serving):

Calories: 235; Fat: 14.4; Carb: 0.83; Protein: 26.03

Salmon with Capers

Prep Time: 15 Minutes
Cook Time: 15 Minutes
Serves: 4

Ingredients:

- 4 (6-ounce) salmon fillets
- Olive oil, for brushing
- 1/2 teaspoon kosher salt, plus more for brining
- 1/2 teaspoon freshly ground black pepper
- 6 lemon slices (from 1 lemon)
- Fresh oregano or thyme sprigs (optional)
- 3 tablespoons salted butter
- 2 tablespoons jarred capers, drained
- 1 garlic clove, grated
- To garnish: finely chopped Italian parsley, chives, or other herbs

Directions:

1. Preheat the oven to 325 degrees Fahrenheit.
2. Brine the salmon: While the oven preheats, in a shallow dish mix together 4 cups room temperature water and 3 tablespoons kosher salt. Place the salmon in the water and wait for 15 minutes.
3. Place the salmon in foil: Place a large sheet of aluminum foil on a baking sheet and brush it with olive oil. Pat each piece of salmon dry and place it on the foil. Sprinkle the salmon with 1/8 teaspoon kosher salt for each fillet and fresh ground pepper. Place the lemon slices and fresh herbs around the salmon (not on top). Close and seal the foil around the salmon.
4. Bake: Bake the salmon for 10 minutes in the foil. Then open the foil packet so steam can release and bake again for 3 to 6 minutes, depending on thickness, until just tender and pink at the center (the internal temperature should be between 125 to 130F in the center). A 1 inch thick fillet should cook in about 15 minutes total.

5. Make the caper butter: Meanwhile, melt the butter over low heat. Once melted, add the capers and garlic and cook until fragrant, about 3 minutes.
6. Serve: When the salmon is done, squeeze with some lemon juice from remaining lemon slices. Spoon the butter sauce over each piece of salmon. Garnish with finely chopped parsley or chives.

Nutritional Value (Amount per Serving):

Calories: 862; Fat: 47.4; Carb: 7.79; Protein: 97.08

Authentic Tzatziki Recipe

Prep Time: 1 Hour 15 Minutes
Cook Time: 0 Minute
Serves: 2

Ingredients:

- 10 ounces cucumber (1 medium cucumber or 3/4 large cucumber)
- 1 garlic clove ● 1 tablespoon chopped fresh dill (do not substitute dried)
- 18 ounces full-fat Greek yogurt ● 1 ½ tablespoons white wine vinegar
- 1 tablespoon olive oil ● ¼ teaspoon kosher salt
- Fresh ground black pepper

Directions:

1. Peel the cucumber, cut it in half, then scoop out the seeds with a spoon. Grate the cucumber using a box grater, then place the shreds in a fine mesh strainer and squeeze out as much liquid as possible. Sprinkle with kosher salt, then let stand for at least 10 minutes to drain any remaining water. Squeeze once more to drain.
2. Mince 1 clove garlic and chop 1 tablespoon fresh dill.
3. When the cucumber is ready, mix cucumber, garlic, dill, 18 ounces Greek yogurt, 1 ½ tablespoons white wine vinegar, 1 tablespoon olive oil, ¼ teaspoon kosher salt, and a few grinds of fresh ground black pepper. Refrigerate for at least 1 to 2 hours so the flavors can marry. Keeps up to 1 week in the refrigerator.

4. To serve, drizzle with olive oil; if desired, garnish with olives and a sprig of dill. Serve with pita, crackers, or vegetables.

Nutritional Value (Amount per Serving):

Calories: 184; Fat: 5.38; Carb: 17.91; Protein: 16.48

Quick Hummus Bowls

Prep Time: 5 Minutes
Cook Time: 0 Minute
Serves: 1

Ingredients:

- ⅓ cup hummus
- 8 English cucumber slices (or standard cucumber, peeled)
- 1 handful red onion slices (or shallot)
- 1 handful cherry tomatoes, sliced   • 1 handful Kalamata olives
- 2 tablespoons feta cheese, to sprinkle (optional or use vegan feta for vegan)   • 1 handful baby greens or chopped lettuce (optional)
- ½ cup cooked rice or packaged pre-cooked rice (optional) or Easy Couscous or Easy Orzo
- 1 pita bread, pita chips, or gluten free crackers
- Optional toppings: Jarred Calabrian chilis or roasted red peppers, caper berries, fresh herbs, frozen or homemade falafel, etc.

Directions:

1. Place greens and rice in the bowl, if using (try packaged pre-cooked rice for a quick shortcut). If using rice, season it with salt and a drizzle of olive oil.
2. Top with hummus, sliced cucumber, sliced red onions, sliced tomatoes, olives and feta cheese. Eat with pita wedges, using the hummus as a dip / dressing for the veggies.

Nutritional Value (Amount per Serving):

Calories: 541; Fat: 26.89; Carb: 73.04; Protein: 21.27

Lemon Dill Salmon

Prep Time: 10 Minutes
Cook Time: 10 Minutes
Serves: 4

Ingredients:

- For the salmon • 4 salmon fillets (skin on or off)
- Kosher salt • Black pepper
- For the lemon dill sauce (makes about ¾ cup)
- 2 tablespoons finely chopped dill
- ¼ cup Greek yogurt
- 6 tablespoons mayonnaise
- 1 tablespoon lemon juice
- ¼ teaspoon garlic powder
- ¼ teaspoon onion powder
- ⅛ teaspoon kosher salt • 2 teaspoons water

Directions:

1. Preheat the oven to 450 degrees Fahrenheit.
2. Generously sprinkle the salmon with kosher salt and fresh ground black pepper. Place it on a parchment-lined baking sheet.
3. Bake the salmon for about 10 minutes until flaky and just cooked; test it with a fork to assess doneness. Watch the salmon to make sure not to overcook; the timing can vary based on the thickness of the salmon and variations between ovens.
4. While the salmon bakes, mix together the sauce ingredients, adding the water last. Use the water to bring it to a loose, drizzle-able consistency. (You may need a touch more depending on your yogurt brand.)
5. Serve the salmon and garnish each fillet with 2 tablespoons of the lemon dill sauce. Save leftover sauce refrigerated.

Nutritional Value (Amount per Serving):
Calories: 727; Fat: 37.64; Carb: 4.52; Protein: 89.22

Baked Shrimp with Feta And Tomatoes

Prep Time: 10 Minutes
Cook Time: 20 Minutes
Serves: 4

Ingredients:

- 1 medium yellow onion
- 2 cloves garlic
- 1 tablespoon olive oil
- 28-ounce can diced fire roasted tomatoes
- ¼ cup fresh parsley, minced
- 1 pound medium raw shrimp, peeled, deveined and shells removed (thawed if frozen)
- 2/3 cup feta crumbled cheese
- ½ teaspoon kosher salt
- Fresh ground pepper
- Lemon

Directions:

1. Preheat oven to 425°F.
2. Finely dice the onion. Mince the garlic.
3. In a large ovenproof skillet over medium-high heat, heat the olive oil. Add the onion and cook until soft, 3-5 minutes. Add the garlic and cook until fragrant, about 30 seconds more. Add the tomatoes and bring to a simmer. Reduce the heat and let the sauce simmer for 5 to 8 minutes, until the juices thicken a bit.
4. While the vegetables cook, mince ¼ cup fresh parsley.
5. Remove the sauce from the heat, and stir in the parsley, shrimp, feta cheese, kosher salt, and several grinds of fresh pepper.
6. Place the skillet in the oven and bake until the shrimp are cooked through, about 8-10 minutes. Garnish with fresh parsley and a squeeze of lemon juice. Serve immediately with bread, rice, quinoa, or couscous.

Nutritional Value (Amount per Serving):

Calories: 230; Fat: 10.48; Carb: 14.14; Protein: 21.35

Mediterranean Couscous Bowls Recipe

Prep Time: 20 Minutes
Cook Time: 5 Minutes
Serves: 4

Ingredients:

- For the chickpeas (or substitute Seasoned Lentils)
- 1 ½ cups cooked or 1 15-ounce can chickpeas (try Instant Pot Chickpeas)
- 1 tablespoon olive oil
- ½ teaspoon cumin
- ½ teaspoon kosher salt
- For the couscous
- 1 cup whole wheat couscous (substitute cooked quinoa for gluten-free)
- ¾ teaspoon kosher salt
- 1 tablespoon olive oil
- 2 tablespoons finely chopped parsley
- For the bowl
- 1 small cucumber
- 1 pint cherry tomatoes
- 8 cups salad greens
- 1 recipe Best Tahini Sauce

Directions:

1. Make the chickpeas: If using dry chickpeas, cook them using our Instant Pot chickpeas method (in under 1 hour!) or our Dutch oven method. If using canned, drain and rinse them. In a medium bowl, stir them together with the olive oil, cumin, and kosher salt.
2. Make the couscous: In a medium pot, bring 1 ¼ cups water to a boil. Add couscous and ½ teaspoon kosher salt. Bring to a boil, then remove from the heat, cover, and let stand for 5 minutes. When done, stir in the olive oil, another ¼ teaspoon kosher salt, and the parsley.
3. Make the dressing: Go to Best Tahini Sauce.

4. Assemble the bowls: Peel and chop the cucumber. Slice the tomatoes in half. In a large shallow bowl, place the greens, then top with couscous, chickpeas, cucumber, and tomatoes. Drizzle with tahini dressing (about 2 tablespoons per bowl). Serve immediately. Leftovers stay in the refrigerator for a few days: keep all components separate for maximum freshness.

Nutritional Value (Amount per Serving):

Calories: 376; Fat: 28.58; Carb: 26.39; Protein: 5.6

Creamy Mushroom Risotto

Prep Time: 20 Minutes
Cook Time: 25 Minutes
Serves: 4 To 6

Ingredients:

- 2 quarts Homemade Mushroom Broth, purchased mushroom broth, or 1 quart vegetable broth, 4 cups water and 1 teaspoon kosher salt
- 1/2 yellow onion
- 1 pound fresh mushrooms: a mix of baby bella (aka cremini), button, shiitake, portobello, oyster, or other
- Kosher salt
- 3 tablespoons salted butter, divided
- 2 tablespoons extra-virgin olive oil
- ¼ teaspoon garlic powder
- 2 cups white arborio rice
- 1 cup dry white wine, such as Pinot Grigio or Chardonnay (optional but recommended)
- 1 cup shredded Parmesan cheese
- For serving: Zest from ½ lemon, freshly ground black pepper, and fresh thyme

Directions:

1. Heat the broth: Make the mushroom broth (our preferred method for best flavor) and start the 15 minute simmer. OR combine 1 quart vegetable

broth, 4 cups water, and 1 teaspoon kosher salt in a saucepan and place it over low heat. The homemade broth only adds a few minutes to the cook time, so we highly recommend it! Simmer it while you complete Step 2, 3 and 4.

2. Cut the vegetables: Finely mince the onion, then place it in a bowl and reserve. Slice the mushrooms (we used a mix of baby bella and baby shiitake).

3. Saute the mushrooms: Add 1 tablespoon of the butter in a large skillet over medium high heat. Add the mushrooms and cook until browned, stirring occasionally: about 5 to 7 minutes depending on mushrooms. Stir in ¼ teaspoon salt, then remove from the pan and set aside.

4. Start the risotto: In the same skillet, heat the olive oil and the remaining 2 tablespoons butter over medium heat. Add the minced onion and cook for about 2 minutes until tender. Add the garlic powder and rice and cook, stirring occasionally, about 2 minutes until the rice starts to turn light brown. Stir in the wine and cook until the liquid is fully absorbed, about 2 minutes.

5. Add the broth: Add two ladles of the hot broth to the risotto. Cook, stirring occasionally until the liquid is fully absorbed, then add two more ladles of both. Cook in this same manner for about 12 minutes, adding two ladles and stirring. Then taste a grain of rice. If it's creamy but still al dente in the center, you're ready for the final step! If not, continue to cook and add broth for a few minutes more. (You may have some broth left over: save it for reheating leftovers.)

6. Finish the risotto: When the rice is al dente, reduce the heat to low. Add two more ladles of broth, the Parmesan cheese and a few grinds of black pepper. Stir vigorously for 1 to 2 minutes until you've got a thick and creamy risotto. Then stir in the sautéed mushrooms. Taste and add additional kosher salt if desired. Serve topped with lemon zest, Parmesan shavings, fresh thyme, and black pepper.

7. Storage info: Flavor is best day of. You can store leftovers refrigerated for up to 3 days, but the texture will become less creamy when chilled. Reheat on the stovetop and add a little extra broth and Parmesan cheese, and a few pinches salt to taste. (See Make Ahead section above for tips.)

Nutritional Value (Amount per Serving):

Calories: 715; Fat: 25.86; Carb: 77.48; Protein: 41.95

Tuscan Soup with White Beans

Prep Time: 10 Minutes
Cook Time: 20 Minutes
Serves: 6 To 8

Ingredients:

- 1 bulb fennel
- 2 bunches Tuscan kale or other dark leafy greens (Swiss chard, spinach, mustard greens)   • 2 15-ounce cans cannellini beans
- 2 tablespoons olive oil
- 2 28-ounce cans diced tomatoes (San Marzano, if possible)
- 4 cups vegetable broth (or canned broth)
- 2 cups water   • ½ teaspoon red pepper flakes
- 1 teaspoon dried basil
- ½ teaspoon smoked paprika
- 1 teaspoon kosher salt
- Pecorino cheese to garnish (optional)

Directions:

1. Chop the fennel bulb (reserve some sprigs for a garnish). Wash and roughly chop the kale. Drain and rinse the cannellini beans.
2. In a large pot or Dutch oven, heat the olive oil over medium high heat, then sauté the fennel for 5 minutes.
3. Add the canned tomatoes with their juices and simmer for 8 minutes.
4. Add the vegetable broth, water and cannellini beans. Bring to a boil.
5. Reduce to a simmer and add the red pepper flakes, dried basil, smoked paprika, and kosher salt.
6. Add the kale and simmer until tender, about 5 minutes. Serve garnished with grated Pecorino cheese and fennel sprigs. Store refrigerated for 3 days or frozen up to 3 months.

Nutritional Value (Amount per Serving):

Calories: 251; Fat: 17.25; Carb: 19.39; Protein: 10.45

Keto Eggplant Parmesan

Prep Time: 15 Minutes
Cook Time: 25 Minutes
Serves: 4

Ingredients:

- 1 medium large eggplant, about 1 pound (long and thin preferable) OR see casserole variation
- 2 eggs
- ½ cup grated Parmesan cheese
- ½ cup almond flour
- 1 tablespoon Italian seasoning (or 1 teaspoon each dried basil, oregano and thyme)
- ¾ teaspoon kosher salt
- 2 cups jarred marinara sauce
- 1 cup grated mozzarella cheese (we used a combination of fresh mozzarella and shredded)
- Fresh basil, to serve

Directions:

1. Preheat the oven to 425 degrees Fahrenheit. Line a baking sheet with parchment paper or spray with cooking spray.
2. Cut off the ends of the eggplant and cut it into 3/8-inch slices.
3. Beat the eggs in a shallow bowl and set it aside.
4. Combine the Parmesan cheese, almond flour, Italian seasoning, and kosher salt in another shallow bowl and set it aside.
5. Dip each eggplant slice into the egg and then the Parmesan cheese mixture. Transfer the coated eggplant slices to the prepared sheet pan in a single layer, about 1/2-inch apart. Use two sheet pans if you do not have one large enough to fit all the slices.
6. Bake the eggplant for about 20 minutes, flipping them halfway through, until tender and golden brown.

7. Remove the eggplant from the oven (go to Casserole Variation if desired). Add 2 tablespoons of the marinara sauce on top of each eggplant slice and add an equal amount of mozzarella cheese on top of the sauce.

8. Return the pan to the oven and continue to bake for 5 to 7 minutes, or until the cheese is melted and the crust is golden brown. Top with torn basil. Serve with pasta (gluten free or legume pasta) or a few side dishes, or the casserole variation makes for a more filling main dish.

Nutritional Value (Amount per Serving):

Calories: 232; Fat: 8.84; Carb: 20.08; Protein: 20.42

Mediterranean Pizza

Prep Time: 1 Hour
Cook Time: 7 Minutes
Serves: 1

Ingredients:

- 1 ball Best Pizza Dough (or Food Processor Dough or Thin Crust Dough)
- ⅓cup Best Homemade Pizza Sauce
- 1 teaspoon olive oil
- 1 cup packed baby spinach leaves
- 1 handful red onion slices
- 6 Kalamata olives
- 8 sundried tomatoes, packed in oil
- ¾ cup shredded mozzarella cheese
- 1 ounce feta cheese
- 8 fresh basil leaves
- Kosher salt
- Semolina flour or cornmeal, for dusting the pizza peel

Directions:

1. Make the pizza dough: Follow the Best Pizza Dough recipe to prepare the

dough. (This takes about 15 minutes to make and 45 minutes to rest.)

2. Place a pizza stone in the oven and preheat to 500°F. OR preheat your pizza oven (here's the pizza oven we use).

3. Make the pizza sauce: Make the 5 Minute Pizza Sauce.

4. Prepare the toppings: In a small skillet, heat the olive oil over medium heat. Add the spinach and cook for 2 minutes until wilted but still bright green. Add 1 pinch salt and remove from the heat.

5. Thinly slice the red onion. Slice the olives in half. If the sundried tomatoes are large, you can chop them smaller too.

6. Bake the pizza: When the oven is ready, dust a pizza peel with cornmeal or semolina flour. (If you don't have a pizza peel, you can use a rimless baking sheet or the back of a rimmed baking sheet. But a pizza peel is well worth the investment!) Stretch the dough into a circle; see How to Stretch Pizza Dough for instructions. Then gently place the dough onto the pizza peel.

7. Spread the pizza sauce over the dough using the back of a spoon to create a thin layer. Add the shredded mozzarella cheese. Top with the cooked spinach, red onion, olives, sundried tomatoes. and feta cheese.

8. Use the pizza peel to carefully transfer the pizza onto the preheated pizza stone. Bake the pizza until the cheese and crust are nicely browned, about 5 to 7 minutes in the oven (or 1 minute in a pizza oven).

9. Allow the pizza to cool for a minute or two before adding the basil on top (whole leaves, lightly torn, or thinly sliced). Slice into pieces and serve immediately.

Nutritional Value (Amount per Serving):

Calories: 732; Fat: 24.18; Carb: 84.67; Protein: 56.41

Ribollita (Tuscan Vegetable Stew)

Prep Time: 10 Minutes
Cook Time: 50 Minutes
Serves: 4

Ingredients:

- 1 onion
- 2 carrots
- 1 zucchini
- 1 tomato
- 4 garlic cloves
- 1 bunch Tuscan kale
- 1 handful parsley
- 2 tablespoons olive oil
- 1 pinch red pepper flakes
- 10 sage leaves
- 15-ounce can cannellini beans (or 1 ½ cups cooked)
- 1 quart vegetable stock
- Kosher salt and fresh ground pepper
- Multigrain or wholegrain sourdough bread
- Parmesan cheese (optional)

Directions:

1. Dice the onion. Peel and dice the carrot and zucchini. Dice the tomato. Mince the garlic. Roughly chop the kale. Remove the leaves from the parsley.
2. In a large saucepan or pot, heat the olive oil. Add the onion garlic, carrots, red pepper flakes, and sage and cook over low heat for 20 minutes until softened but not browned. Add the parsley, tomato, and zucchini and cook for a few minutes.
3. Add the kale and beans (drained if canned), and cover with vegetable stock. Bring to a boil, reduce the heat and simmer for 30 minutes. Season with kosher salt and fresh ground black pepper to taste.
4. Chop the bread into cubes. To serve, arrange the bread cubes in the soup and add Parmesan cheese shavings and a drizzle of olive oil.

Nutritional Value (Amount per Serving):

Calories: 193; Fat: 11.86; Carb: 20.61; Protein: 4.91

Easy Mussels Marinara

Prep Time: 5 Minutes
Cook Time: 20 Minutes
Serves: 4

Ingredients:

- 1 recipe Easy Marinara Sauce (28 ounces)
- 8 ounces spaghetti or bucatini pasta
- 1 1/2 pounds mussels
- To serve: Chopped fresh basil (left over from the marinara), olive oil

Directions:

1. Start the Easy Marinara Sauce.
2. Clean the mussels (see the section above).
3. Bring a large pot of salted water to a boil. Boil the pasta until it is al dente (start tasting a few minutes before the package recommends: you want it to be tender but still a little firm on the inside). Then drain.
4. After the marinara sauce has simmered for 15 minutes, add the mussels and cook covered over medium heat for 6 to 8 minutes until they open. Stirring several times.
5. To serve, place pasta in a dish and spoon mussels and marinara over the pasta. Garnish with chopped basil and a drizzle of olive oil.

Nutritional Value (Amount per Serving):

Calories: 194; Fat: 4.77; Carb: 15.2; Protein: 22.11

Burrata Pasta With Tomato Basil

Prep Time: 10 Minutes
Cook Time: 15 Minutes
Serves: 4

Ingredients:

- ¼ cup olive oil   • 4 medium garlic cloves, peeled and sliced
- 28 ounce whole San Marzano tomatoes   • 1 teaspoon kosher salt
- ½ cup roughly chopped basil leaves, plus more for garnish
- 8 ounces spaghetti or bucatini pasta
- ½ pint red and yellow cherry tomatoes, sliced in half (or, omit if they're not in season)   • ¼ cup grated Parmesan cheese
- 8 ounces (2 balls) burrata cheese
- Fresh ground black pepper, for serving (optional)

Directions:

1. Make the tomato basil sauce: Add the olive oil to a saucepan over medium heat. Add the sliced garlic and cook for about 30 to 45 seconds until lightly browned and fragrant. Add the whole tomatoes with the can liquid, taking care as it may spit as the tomatoes hit the hot oil. Use a potato masher to break up the tomatoes into small pieces (see the sauce photo above). Add the kosher salt and chopped basil leaves and bring to a heavy simmer. Cover the saucepan with a lid slightly ajar and simmer, bubbling rapidly, for 10 to 12 minutes until thickened. (If you prefer a smoother texture you can immersion blend it, but we highly recommend the chunky rustic texture here.)
2. Cook the pasta: Meanwhile, bring a large pot of heavily salted water to a boil. Add the pasta and cook until al dente. Set the timer for a few minutes less than the package instructions and then taste: the pasta should be just done, still with some firmness. Drain the pasta and return to the pot. Add a drizzle of olive oil if the sauce is not yet done, to prevent sticking.

3.Serve: Toss the noodles with the sauce until well coated. Add to a platter and top with the grated Parmesan. Add the two burrata balls, and arrange the cherry tomatoes around them. Top with a drizzle of olive oil, several pinches kosher salt, fresh ground black pepper and additional chopped basil. When serving, have each eater break off pieces of the burrata for their portion, or simply break it into pieces and lightly toss throughout the pasta.

Nutritional Value (Amount per Serving):

Calories: 384; Fat: 28.7; Carb: 20.09; Protein: 14.31

Bruschetta Steak

Prep Time: 10 Minutes
Cook Time: 15 Minutes
Serves: 4

Ingredients:

- 3 medium tomatoes, chopped
- 3 tablespoons minced fresh basil
- 3 tablespoons chopped fresh parsley
- 2 tablespoons olive oil
- 1 teaspoon minced fresh oregano or 1/2 teaspoon dried oregano
- 1 garlic clove, minced
- 3/4 teaspoon salt, divided
- 1 beef flat iron or top sirloin steak (1 pound), cut into four portions
- 1/4 teaspoon pepper
- Grated Parmesan cheese, optional

Directions:

1. Combine first 6 ingredients; stir in 1/4 teaspoon salt.
2. Sprinkle beef with pepper and remaining salt. Grill, covered, over medium heat or broil 4 in. from heat until meat reaches desired doneness (for medium-rare, a thermometer should read 135°F; medium, 140°F), 4-6 minutes per side. Top with tomato mixture. If desired, sprinkle with cheese.

Nutritional Value (Amount per Serving):

Calories: 367; Fat: 23.87; Carb: 4.86; Protein: 32.15

Elegant Pork Marsala

Prep Time: 10 Minutes
Cook Time: 20 Minutes
Serves: 6

Ingredients:

- 1/3 cup whole wheat flour
- 1/2 teaspoon pepper
- 6 boneless pork loin chops (4 ounces each)
- 1 tablespoon olive oil
- 2 cups sliced fresh mushrooms
- 1/3 cup chopped onion
- 2 turkey bacon strips, chopped
- 1/4 teaspoon minced garlic
- 1 cup Marsala wine or additional reduced-sodium chicken broth
- 5 teaspoons cornstarch
- 2/3 cup reduced-sodium chicken broth

Directions:

1. In a shallow bowl, mix flour and pepper. Dip pork chops in flour mixture to coat both sides; shake off excess.
2. In a large nonstick skillet, heat oil over medium heat. Add pork chops; cook 4-5 minutes on each side or until a thermometer reads 145°. Remove from pan; keep warm.
3. In same skillet, add mushrooms, onion and bacon to drippings; cook and stir 2-3 minutes or until mushrooms are tender. Add garlic; cook 1 minute longer. Add wine; increase heat to medium-high. Cook, stirring to loosen browned bits from pan.
4. 4. In a small bowl, mix cornstarch and broth until smooth; add to pan. Bring to a boil; cook and stir 2 minutes or until slightly thickened. Serve with pork.

Nutritional Value (Amount per Serving):

Calories: 595; Fat: 32.7; Carb: 17.47; Protein: 59.33

Pesto Corn Salad With Shrimp

Prep Time: 10 Minutes
Cook Time: 20 Minutes
Serves: 4

Ingredients:

- 4 medium ears sweet corn, husked
- 1/2 cup packed fresh basil leaves
- 1/4 cup olive oil
- 1/2 teaspoon salt, divided
- 1-1/2 cups cherry tomatoes, halved
- 1/8 teaspoon pepper
- 1 medium ripe avocado, peeled and chopped
- 1 pound uncooked shrimp (31-40 per pound), peeled and deveined

Directions:

1. In a pot of boiling water, cook corn until tender, about 5 minutes. Drain; cool slightly. Meanwhile, in a food processor, pulse basil, oil and 1/4 teaspoon salt until blended.
2. Cut corn from cob and place in a bowl. Stir in tomatoes, pepper and remaining 1/4 teaspoon salt. Add avocado and 2 tablespoons basil mixture; toss gently to combine.
3. Thread shrimp onto metal or soaked wooden skewers; brush with remaining basil mixture. Grill, covered, over medium heat until shrimp turn pink, 2-4 minutes per side. Remove shrimp from skewers; serve with corn mixture.

Nutritional Value (Amount per Serving):

Calories: 453; Fat: 24.15; Carb: 35.72; Protein: 29.15

Mediterranean Turkey Skillet

Prep Time: 10 Minutes

Cook Time: 20 Minutes

Serves: 6

Ingredients:

- 1 tablespoon olive oil
- 1 package (20 ounces) lean ground turkey
- 2 medium zucchini, quartered lengthwise and cut into 1/2-inch slices
- 1 medium onion, chopped
- 2 banana peppers, seeded and chopped
- 3 garlic cloves, minced
- 1/2 teaspoon dried oregano
- 1 can (15 ounces) black beans, rinsed and drained
- 1 can (14-1/2 ounces) diced tomatoes, undrained
- 1 tablespoon balsamic vinegar
- 1/2 teaspoon salt

Directions:

1. In a large skillet, heat oil over medium-high heat. Add turkey, zucchini, onion, peppers, garlic and oregano; cook 10-12 minutes or until turkey is no longer pink and vegetables are tender, breaking up turkey into crumbles; drain. Stir in remaining ingredients; heat through, stirring occasionally.

Nutritional Value (Amount per Serving):

Calories: 175; Fat: 4.16; Carb: 33.4; Protein: 4.63

Chapter 4: Drink

Simple Green Juice Recipe

Prep Time: 15 Minutes
Cook Time: 0 Minute
Serves: 2

Ingredients:

- 1 bunch kale (about 5 oz)
- 1 inch piece fresh ginger, peeled
- 1 Granny smith apple (or any large apple)
- 5 celery stalks, ends trimmed
- ½ large English cucumber
- Handful fresh parsley (about 1 oz)

Directions:

1. Wash and prep the vegetables. I like to cut them in large chunks.
2. Juice in the order listed (or add them to a blender and blend on high.)
3. If you used a juicer, simply pour the green juice into glasses and enjoy immediately. If you used a blender, the juice will be thicker. You can pour it through a fine mesh sieve, and using the back of a spoon, press the pulp into the sieve to extract as much liquid as possible. Pour the strained juice into glasses and enjoy!

Nutritional Value (Amount per Serving):

Calories: 129; Fat: 1.25; Carb: 27.5; Protein: 4.27

Italian Hot Chocolate (Cioccolato Caldo)

Prep Time: 5 Minutes
Cook Time: 5 Minutes
Serves: 6

Ingredients:

- 6 ounces dark chocolate 70-74%, chopped small
- 2 teaspoons granulated sugar
- 4 tablespoons unsweetened cocoa powder
- 1 tablespoon cornstarch
- pinch of salt
- 2 cups 2% milk
- chocolate shavings for garnish, optional

Directions:

1. Combine the dry ingredients: In a small bowl, combine the dark chocolate, sugar, cocoa powder, cornstarch, and salt. Set aside.
2. Warm the milk: Pour the milk into a medium saucepan over medium-low heat, and bring to a simmer (watch for bubbles forming around the edges).
3. Add the dry ingredients to the milk: Dump the dry ingredients into the simmering milk and stir with a wooden spoon or heat-proof spatula until the chocolate is melted and smooth, 4-5 minutes.
4. Let cool: Remove from heat and let cool for 5 minutes. If any skin starts to appear on the surface, whisk the mixture.
5. Serve: Pour into heat-proof cups. Garnish with chocolate shavings and/or whipped cream if desired. Serve immediately.

Nutritional Value (Amount per Serving):

Calories: 254; Fat: 15.29; Carb: 25.28; Protein: 5.56

Mediterranean Herb Mix

Prep Time: 5 Minutes
Cook Time: 0 Minute
Serves: 12

Ingredients:

- 2 tablespoons dried oregano
- 2 tablespoons dried rosemary
- 2 tablespoons dried thyme
- 1 tablespoon dried mint
- 1 tablespoon dried sage

Directions:

1. Combine oregano, rosemary, thyme, mint, and sage in a clean glass jar with a tight-fitting lid. Secure the lid and shake until the seasonings are mixed well. Store in a cool, dry place (or the fridge) for up to 6 months. Just before using, crush the herbs between your fingers, with a mortar and pestle, or in a spice mill to release their flavors.
2. To make ahead: Store in an airtight container at room temperature or in the refrigerator for up to 6 months.

Nutritional Value (Amount per Serving):

Calories: 2; Fat: 0.07; Carb: 0.53; Protein: 0.1

Chapter 5: Snack

Classic Gazpacho

Prep Time: 10 Minutes
Cook Time: 0 Minute
Serves: 4

Ingredients:

- 2 pounds ripe quality tomatoes, cored and roughly chopped (about 3 large)
- 1/2 medium cucumber, peeled and roughly chopped
- 1/2 red bell pepper, roughly chopped
- 1 tablespoon minced shallot
- 1 small garlic clove, peeled
- 1/4 cup olive oil
- 2 tablespoons sherry vinegar (or red wine vinegar)
- 3/4 teaspoon kosher salt
- 1/4 teaspoon smoked paprika (pimenton)

Directions:

1. Place all ingredients in a blender, and blend until smooth. Taste and adjust salt as needed.
2. Refrigerate until cold, about 2 hours, or up to 3 days before serving.
3. Serve topped with additional chopped veggies, a drizzle of olive oil, and toasted bread.

Nutritional Value (Amount per Serving):

Calories: 170; Fat: 14.04; Carb: 10.68; Protein: 2.38

Eggplant Caponata

Prep Time: 10 Minutes
Cook Time: 25 Minutes
Serves: 6

Ingredients:

- 1 1/2 pounds eggplant (2 medium)
- 1 celery rib
- 1 medium red onion
- 1/2 red bell pepper
- 3 garlic cloves
- ¼ cup olive oil
- 14-ounce can crushed fire roasted tomatoes
- 2 tablespoons balsamic vinegar
- 1 tablespoon sugar
- 1 pinch red pepper flakes
- 2 tablespoons capers, drained
- ½ teaspoon kosher salt
- Basil, for garnish
- Toasted pine nuts, for garnish (optional)

Directions:

1. Cut the eggplant into small cubes, about ½ inch by ½ inch. Dice the celery. Slice the red onion. Dice the red bell pepper. Mince the garlic.
2. In a Dutch oven or large saute pan, heat the olive oil over medium heat.
3. Add the eggplant, celery, red pepper and red onion and cook for 10 minutes, stirring occasionally. Add the garlic and cook 3 to 5 minutes until the eggplant and onions are browned and softened.
4. Add the crushed tomatoes, balsamic vinegar, sugar, red pepper flakes, capers, and salt. Cover and simmer on low for 10 minutes, stirring once, until very tender. Taste and add another pinch or two of salt. Serve warm, garnished with chopped basil and toasted pine nuts. Or, chill for up to 1 day and serve cold or at room temperature (the flavors taste even better after refrigerating).

Nutritional Value (Amount per Serving):

Calories: 147; Fat: 9.53; Carb: 15.2; Protein: 2.49

Greek Fries

Prep Time: 15 Minutes
Cook Time: 30 Minutes
Serves: 3 To 4

Ingredients:

- 6 medium Yukon gold potatoes (1 1/2 to 1 3/4 pounds)
- 2 tablespoons olive oil
- 1 tablespoon homemade Greek Seasoning
- ½ teaspoon kosher salt
- ¼ cup feta crumbles
- 2 tablespoons finely chopped curly parsley
- 2 tablespoons finely chopped red onion
- 4 lemon wedges, for serving
- Optional: tzatziki, lemon dill sauce (our favorite), or aioli, for dipping

Directions:

1. Preheat the oven to 425 degrees Fahrenheit. Evenly space the oven racks to ensure even cooking.
2. Meanwhile, cut the potatoes into fries: (Watch this video or use a fry cutter.) Wash the potatoes, leaving the skins on. Slice off the ends of each potato, then slice off part of the side to make a base. Place the potato half cut side down and cut off a 3/8-inch slice, then lay the slice on its side and cut it into several long strips. Repeat until all potatoes have been cut into fries. The pieces can be uneven, but aim for as uniform of thickness as possible. See the video for full instructions!
3. Soak in cold water (10 minutes): Place the cut fries into a medium bowl and rinse with cold water until water is clear. Then fill the bowl with cold water and allow to rest for 10 minutes (while the oven preheats). Then drain the potatoes and dry them thoroughly with a clean dish towel.
4. Season the fries: Add the fries to a dry bowl and toss them with the olive oil, Greek seasoning and kosher salt. Line two baking sheets with

paper. Spread the fries in straight lines on the paper, placing them as far apart as possible.

5. Bake: Bake the fries for 20 minutes. Take them out of the oven and carefully flip each fry. Return to oven (reversing the pans on top and bottom racks). Bake additional 8 to 10 minutes until they are crisp and golden brown, watching carefully as the bake time depends on the fry thickness and your oven. (If the majority of the fries seem soft, continue to bake a few more minutes.)

6. Season: Taste and add a few more pinches salt if desired.

7. Garnish: Transfer fries to a platter and top with the feta cheese crumbles, breaking larger chunks into small pieces with your fingers. Add the finely chopped parsley and red onion. Serve with lemon wedges and tzatziki or lemon dill sauce.

Nutritional Value (Amount per Serving):

Calories: 553; Fat: 11.83; Carb: 102.26; Protein: 12.92

Baked Feta With Tomatoes

Prep Time: 5 Minutes
Cook Time: 18 Minutes
Serves: 4

Ingredients:

- 8 to 10 cherry tomatoes
- 1 garlic clove
- 2 tablespoons fresh parsley
- 10 Kalamata olives
- 4 to 5 ounce block of feta cheese
- 1 tablespoon olive oil
- ½ teaspoon dried oregano
- Kosher salt

Directions:

1. Preheat the oven to 400ºF.
2. Slice the cherry tomatoes in half and add a few pinches kosher salt. Finely mince the garlic. Chop the parsley.
3. In a small oven-proof dish, place the tomatoes, garlic, parsley, and Kalamata olives, then top with the feta cheese. Drizzle with the olive oil and sprinkle with the dried oregano.
4. Bake for about 18 minutes, until the feta cheese is warm and soft. Serve immediately with crackers, pita, or bread.

Nutritional Value (Amount per Serving):

Calories: 521; Fat: 31.91; Carb: 49.92; Protein: 13.21

10-Min Burrata With Tomato, Basil, And Prosciutto

Prep Time: 10 Minutes
Cook Time: 10 Minutes
Serves: 6

Ingredients:

- 8 ounces crusty Italian-style bread, like ciabatta
- Extra virgin olive oil, Italian Nocellara
- 8 ounces burrata cheese
- 3 ounces prosciutto
- 1 cup grape or cherry tomatoes, halved
- 1 Jalapeno, seeded and minced
- 3 ounces sun-dried tomatoes, chopped
- ⅓cup olives, any kind you like
- 2 teaspoons capers
- Basil leaves, handful, torn
- Kosher salt and black pepper
- Red pepper flakes

Directions:

1. Tear the bread up into pieces and arrange them, crusty side down, on a sheet pan. Drizzle with extra virgin olive oil, making sure to spread the evoo over the soft (fleshy) side of the bread. Broil for a couple of minutes, watching carefully for the bread to gain some color.
2. Arrange the toasted bread pieces on a large platter. Add in the burrata, prosciutto and tomatoes, and top with the remaining ingredients.
3. Finish with a good dash of kosher salt and black pepper (particularly on the tomatoes and burrata), and a little red pepper flakes, if you don't mind the heat. Drizzle olive oil all over and serve.

Nutritional Value (Amount per Serving):

Calories: 148; Fat: 9.98; Carb: 8.66; Protein: 7.2

Patata Bravas - Spanish Fried Potatoes

Prep Time: 5 Minutes
Cook Time: 30 Minutes
Serves: 6

Ingredients:

- ¾ teaspoon baking soda
- 4 to 5 Russet potatoes, about 2 pounds, peeled and cut into large 2-inch chunks   • Kosher salt
- Extra virgin olive oil, or a healthy natural cooking oil of your choice
- o Serve: • 1 Homemade Bravas Sauce Recipe
- 1 Garlic aioli of your choice, store-bought is fine, optional

Directions:

1. Fill a medium saucepan with water and bring it to a boil.
2. As soon as the water boils, add the baking soda (it will foam a little). Carefully add the potatoes and allow the water to come to a boil. Boil the potatoes for about 1 to 2 minutes (no longer). Drain the potatoes well in a colander.
3. Transfer the potatoes to a large sheet pan and season them well with kosher salt. Toss to make sure the salt is well distributed, then be sure to spread the potatoes in one single layer.
4. Set the potatoes aside or transfer to the fridge to cool completely (you can do this ahead of time and leave the potatoes in the fridge overnight, but it's important for them to cool completely).
5. In a medium skillet, heat 1 cup of the oil over medium-high heat. When the oil begins to bubble gently, add one piece of potato to test, if the oil around it bubbles a lot, it is ready. Add the rest of the potatoes and spread them out well. You may need to do this in batches so as to not crowd the pan. Cook in the oil, tossing occasionally and making sure the potatoes are well-coated in the oil, until they are golden brown on all sides, about 20 to 25 minutes. Watch them carefully, as they can go from perfectly cooked to burned in a short time.

6. While the potatoes are cooking, work on the bravas sauce (if you did not make it ahead of time).

7. Using a slotted spoon, transfer the potatoes to a tray lined with paper towels to drain excess oil. Immediately season with another pinch of kosher salt.

8. Finish with a good drizzle of bravas sauce and aioli of your choice (if using). Serve immediately with more bravas sauce to the side.

Nutritional Value (Amount per Serving):

Calories: 276; Fat: 0.68; Carb: 62.34; Protein: 7.96

Easy Homemade Frozen Yogurt Recipe

Prep Time: 6 Hours 5 Minutes
Cook Time: 0 Minute
Serves: 6

Ingredients:

- 4 cups sliced frozen strawberries, or other frozen fruit of your choice (see notes)   • 2 cups sliced frozen banana   • 1 cup Whole milk Greek yogurt
- 2 teaspoon orange extract, or vanilla extract, if you like
- 4 to 6 tablespoon honey, more to your liking, I used Greek honey
- ¼ cup sugar, optional but highly recommended
- 1 tablespoon corn syrup, optional

Directions:

1. Combine the frozen strawberries, banana, yogurt, orange extract (or vanilla extract), honey, sugar, and corn syrup in the bowl of a food processor fitted with a blade or a heavy duty blender.

2. Blend until everything is combined into a creamy smoothie-like mixture. Taste, and if you like it sweeter add a bit more honey.

3. Transfer the mixture to a freezer safe container and smooth the surface. Press a piece of parchment against the top of the yogurt to prevent ice crystals from forming. Freeze for at least 6 hours or overnight.

4. To serve, allow the frozen yogurt to sit at room temperature for a few minutes just until soft enough to scoop. Scoop the amount you need (long, shallow pulls or strokes will produce better scoops). Enjoy!

Nutritional Value (Amount per Serving):

Calories: 262; Fat: 2.1; Carb: 63.49; Protein: 3.4

Easy Antipasto Skewers

Prep Time: 20 Minutes
Cook Time: 0 Minute
Serves: 10

Ingredients:

- 10 mini wooden skewers • 10 leaves fresh basil, mint, or flat-leaf parsley
- 10 pieces prosciutto di parma (2 inches in length each), rolled or folded
- 10 pieces preserved artichoke hearts
- 10 mini mozzarella cheese balls, or any firm enough mild cheese
- 10 pitted Kalamata olives   • 10 cherry tomatoes
- pinch dried oregano for garnish • extra virgin olive oil, optional

Directions:

1. Soak mini wooden skewers in water for one hour. Pat dry before using.
2. Skewer the antipasto ingredients beginning perhaps with the basil or parsley, followed by the larger pieces like prosciutto or artichoke hearts. Place the Kalmata olive at the very top of the skewer. If you have more basil or parsley leaves, alternate them on the skewer.
3. Arrange skewers on a serving platter or slate board. If you like, finish with a sprinkle of dried oregano and drizzle of extra virgin olive oil. Serve cold or at room temperature.

Nutritional Value (Amount per Serving):

Calories: 499; Fat: 20.33; Carb: 62.88; Protein: 23.06

Easy Grilled Zucchini

Prep Time: 2 Minutes
Cook Time: 8 Minutes
Serves: 6

Ingredients:

- 3 medium zucchini, halved, then cut into spears (you should end up with 4 long spears per zucchini)
- Kosher salt and black pepper
- Seasoning of your choice, I used 1 teaspoon of dried oregano and 1 teaspoon of sumac
- Extra virgin olive oil   • ½ lemon, juice of

Directions:

1. Place the zucchini spears in a large bowl. Add the kosher salt, black pepper, and seasonings. Drizzle with 2 tablespoons extra virgin olive oil and toss to combine, making sure all the spears are well-coated with the seasoning.
2. Lightly oil the grates of an outdoor grill or indoor griddle and heat over medium-high.
3. When your grill or griddle is hot, arrange the zucchini spears flesh-side down on one of its sides. Grill until you see some deep char marks (about 4 minutes or so), then flip the zucchini over so the skin side is now touching the hot grates. Grill for 4 to 5 minutes, then turn the zucchini one last time over on the other side of the spear (the side that is not charred yet). Grill for a couple more minutes.
4. Remove the spears from the heat and arrange them on a platter. Immediately squeeze half a lemon all over, and if you've used sumac (which I highly recommend) sprinkle a generous amount to finish. Serve immediately.

Nutritional Value (Amount per Serving):

Calories: 15; Fat: 1.05; Carb: 1.27; Protein: 0.34

Chapter 6: Dessert

Easy Baklava Recipe: Baklava Bites

Prep Time: 20 Minutes
Cook Time: 20 Minutes
Serves: 12

Ingredients:

- For the phyllo cups
- 5 sheets phyllo dough
- 1 tablespoon butter
- For the baklava bites
- ½ cup walnuts
- ½ cup pistachios
- 1 tablespoon butter
- 3 tablespoons honey, plus more for serving
- ¼ teaspoon ground cinnamon
- Pinch of kosher salt
- 12 phyllo cups (above, or purchased)

Directions:

1. Make the phyllo cups: Preheat the oven to 375°F. Melt the tablespoon butter. On a clean workspace, place 1 phyllo sheet, taking care to handle it delicately. Using a pastry brush, gently brush the top with butter. Carefully place the next sheet on top of the first sheet (as exact as possible), smooth it out, and brush the top with butter. Repeat for all 5 sheets, brushing the top sheet with butter as well.
2. With a pizza cutter, cut the large piece of layered phyllo dough into 12 rectangles by cutting the long side into 4 even strips and the short side into 3 even strips (trim off rough edges if necessary).
3. Take each rectangle and mold it into the cup of a mini muffin tin. Bake for 10 minutes, until golden. Remove from the oven and let cool slightly.
4. Make the baklava bites: Chop the walnuts and the pistachios. Melt the butter. In a medium bowl, stir together the chopped nuts, melted butter,

honey, cinnamon and a pinch of kosher salt until evenly combined. Place the nut filling evenly into each cup.

5. Bake the cups for 10 minutes, or until the nuts are fragrant and lightly toasted. Remove and drizzle with extra honey before serving. Serve immediately.

Nutritional Value (Amount per Serving):

Calories: 164; Fat: 8.04; Carb: 20.4; Protein: 3.5

Orange Cardamom Olive Oil Cake

Prep Time: 15 Minutes
Cook Time: 40 Minutes
Serves: 12

Ingredients:

- 1 cup extra-virgin olive oil, fruity, more neutral-tasting, plus extra for the pan
- 2 cups all-purpose flour, plus more for the pan
- 1 teaspoon kosher salt
- 1 teaspoon baking powder
- ¼ teaspoon baking soda
- ¾ to 1 teaspoon ground cardamom
- 1 ½ cups plus 2 Tablespoons granulated sugar
- 3 large eggs
- Grated zest of 2 oranges, plus 2 tablespoons fresh orange juice
- 1 ¼ cups whole milk or plant-based alternative
- 2 tablespoons sifted confectioners' sugar, for garnish

Directions:

1. Prepare the oven: Position a rack in the center of the oven and preheat the oven to 350°F.
2. Prepare the baking pan: Brush the bottom and sides of a 9-inch round

cake pan with a little olive oil. Line the bottom of the pan with a round of parchment paper and dust with a bit of the flour, shaking out the excess.

3. Mix together dry ingredients: In a medium bowl, whisk together 2 cups flour, salt, baking powder, and baking soda.

4. Beat the wet ingredients with sugar: In a large bowl, combine the 1 ½ cups granulated sugar, cardamom, and eggs. Using an electric hand mixer set on high, beat the mixture until thick and fluffy, about 5 minutes (or use a stand mixer on high speed). While the mixer is running, slowly drizzle in the olive oil and beat until incorporated. Reduce the speed to low and add half the orange zest, the orange juice, and milk. Beat until smooth.

5. Combine the wet and dry ingredients: Add the flour mixture to wet ingredients and mix on low just until you have a uniform batter.

6. Bake the cake: Pour the cake batter into the pan and sprinkle the top with the remaining 2 tablespoons granulated sugar. Bake the cake for 40 to 45 minutes, or until the center is set and a skewer inserted into the middle comes out clean (ovens do vary, so check your cake at 30 minutes and go from there).

7. Cool the cake: Allow the cake to cool for 30 minutes in the pan, then run a small knife around the edge, invert the cake onto a large plate, then invert again onto a rack to cool completely.

8. Serve: Before serving, dust the cake with powdered sugar and sprinkle with orange zest.

Nutritional Value (Amount per Serving):

Calories: 337; Fat: 21.6; Carb: 32.11; Protein: 4.09

5-Minute Pumpkin Parfait

Prep Time: 5 Minutes
Cook Time: 0 Minute
Serves: 6

Ingredients:

- 1 15-ounce can pumpkin puree, or scant 2 cups homemade pumpkin puree
- 1 ¼ cup Greek yogurt
- 3-4 tablespoons mascarpone cheese
- 1 tablespoon vanilla extract
- 2 ½ tablespoons brown sugar
- 1 ½-2 teaspoons ground cinnamon
- ¼ teaspoon nutmeg
- arfait Toppings
- 2 tablespoons honey or molasses, more for garnish
- Chocolate chips for garnish
- Chopped hazelnuts or walnuts for garnish

Directions:

1. Place the pumpkin puree, Greek yogurt and the remaining ingredients, except the chocolate chips and nuts, in a large mixing bowl. Using a hand electric mixer or a whisk, mix together until you reach a smooth consistency.
2. Give it a taste and adjust flavor to your liking (add a bit of molasses or brown sugar to sweeten some more, for example. Or adjust the spices if you want more cinnamon or nutmeg.) Mix again to combine.
3. Transfer the pumpkin-yogurt mixture to small (3-ounce) serving goblets or small mason jars. Cover and refrigerate for 30 minutes or overnight.
4. When ready to serve, top each with a drizzle of molasses, chocolate chips and chopped hazelnuts or walnuts. Enjoy!

Nutritional Value (Amount per Serving):

Calories: 529; Fat: 28.05; Carb: 52.72; Protein: 21.26

Quick Berry Compote Recipe

Prep Time: 5 Minutes
Cook Time: 25 Minutes
Serves: 56

Ingredients:

- 12 ounces fresh strawberries, hulled and chopped
- 12 ounces fresh blueberries
- 12 ounces fresh raspberries
- 3 tablespoons raw cane sugar
- Juice of 1 lime, optional (you can start with juice of ½ lime)

Directions:

Stovetop Method:

1. Combine the strawberries, blueberries, and raspberries in a medium saucepan or pot. Add the sugar and lime juice. Toss to combine.
2. Bring the mixture to a boil over medium-high heat, stirring occasionally, for about 5 minutes.
3. Once the berry mixture is boiling and the sugar has dissolved, turn the heat down to low (the lowest setting on your stovetop). Allow the berries to simmer for about 15 to 20 minutes, stirring often, until the fruit has softened quite a bit and the compote has reduced by about ½ half in volume.
4. Remove from the heat. At this point, you can use the back of a fork or a potato masher to mash the fruit some more, if you like a smoother compote (I like to see chunks of fruit in mine). You can also carefully taste to adjust sweetness. I don't usually have a need for adding more sugar, but if you need to, you can sprinkle a little more cane sugar or drizzle some honey. Be sure to mix well.
5. Let the berry compote cool for about 15 to 30 minutes before serving. It will thicken some more.
6. See storage instructions below.

Oven Method (Roasted):

1. Heat the oven to 375 degrees F.
2. In a large bowl, combine the chopped strawberries, blueberries, and raspberries. Add in the sugar and lime juice. Toss to coat the fruit with the sugar and lime juice.
3. Transfer the fruit mixture to a large baking dish or a heavy, rimmed sheet pan making sure to spread the fruit well in a single layer.
4. Roast in the heated oven for 30 to 45 minutes, checking every 10 to 15 minutes until the berries have fully collapsed and released some juices. You may like to pull the baking dish out occasionally to give the fruit a stir.
5. Let the roasted berries cool for about 15 to 20 minutes before serving.
6. See storage instructions.

Nutritional Value (Amount per Serving):

Calories: 230; Fat: 1.46; Carb: 56.48; Protein: 2.92

Healthy Carrot Cake Recipe With

Prep Time: 10 Minutes
Cook Time: 1 Hour
Serves: 12

Ingredients:

- 1/2 cup Private Reserve Greek extra virgin olive oil
- 1/2 cup Greek yogurt (reduced fat)
- 1/3 cup milk (2% reduced fat milk)
- 1/2 cup quality dark honey
- 3 eggs at room temperature
- 2 1/4 cup whole wheat flour
- 1 1/2 tsp baking powder
- 1/2 tsp salt

- 4 tsp ground cinnamon
- 1/2 tsp ground cardamom
- 1/4 tsp ground ginger
- 2 cups finely grated carrots (you can use food processor to very finely chop instead)
- 6 Medjool dates, pitted and finely chopped (you can use food processor)
- 1/3 cup chopped walnuts
- powdered sugar for light dusting

Directions:

1. Preheat oven to 350 degrees F.
2. In a large bowl, whisk the olive oil, geek yogurt, and milk. Add eggs one-by-one and whisk to combine.
3. In a separate bowl, whisk flour, baking powder, salt, and spices
4. Gradually add the dry ingredients to the wet ingredients, mixing with a wooden spoon.
5. Fold in the carrots. Mix to combine, then add the dates and walnuts. Again, mix with your wooden spoon until well combined.
6. Line a 9-inch square baking pan like this one with parchment paper (or coat well with olive oil). Pour the carrot cake batter into the pan.
7. Bake in 350 degrees F heated-oven for 1 hour (until a tooth pick inserted in middle of the cake comes out clean). Let cool completely. Sprinkle powdered sugar, if desired. Cut into 9 or 12 square pieces. Enjoy!

Nutritional Value (Amount per Serving):

Calories: 279; Fat: 10.8; Carb: 41.96; Protein: 7.15

Maamoul (Date Filled Cookies)

Prep Time: 45 Minutes
Cook Time: 15 Minutes
Serves: 18

Ingredients:

- ¾ cup ghee or clarified butter
- 3 tablespoons granulated sugar
- 1 large egg, room temperature
- 2 teaspoons orange blossom water, or vanilla extract
- 1 ¼ cups semolina flour
- 1 ¼ cups all-purpose flour, plus more as needed to finish the dough and coat the molds, if using
- 2 teaspoons mahleb, optional; replace with flour if not using
- 1-3 tablespoons milk, any fat content level, at room temperature
- ¼ cup confectioners' sugar, for finishing
- 10 oz date paste, or 20 pureed pitted Medjool dates

Directions:

1. Preheat the oven: Preheat the oven to 350° F. Line two sheet pans with parchment paper.
2. Whisk clarified butter (or ghee), sugar, eggs and blossom water together: In a stand mixer fitted with the whisk attachment or using a hand-held mixer, beat the butter first on medium, then on high speed in a large bowl until creamy and light, about 3 minutes. Scrape down the sides of the bowl and add the sugar, egg, and orange blossom water or vanilla extract. Beat until the mixture is thick, pale, and creamy, another 2-3 minutes, scraping down the sides of the bowl once or twice during beating..
3. Add the flours and mahleb: If using a stand mixer, remove the bowl from the stand. Add the semolina, all-purpose flour. If using mahleb, add that here too. Use a spoon or rubber spatula to combine the ingredients together until you have a crumbly dough that will hold together when squeezed.

4. Check the dough: If the dough stays on your fingertips when squeezed, it is too wet. Add all-purpose flour 1 tablespoon at a time, stir and squeeze. If the dough feels dry (you'll see cracking), add milk 1 tablespoon at a time, stir and squeeze. Squeeze the dough as you work, until the dough is smooth, pliable, and soft.

5. Let the dough rest: Set the dough aside to rest for about 15 minutes, so the flour can absorb the moisture. Test the dough after resting to be sure it is soft and pliable, adding more flour or milk if needed (another rest after this is not necessary).

6. To shape and bake the dough: Take a 1 ounce piece of dough about the size of a walnut or 1 tablespoon, shape into a ball by rolling the dough between the palms of your hands.

7. To shape maamoul using a mold: Coat the interior of the mold with flour and knock out the excess. Do this before molding each cookie to help release the molded dough. Place the dough ball into the mold and press into the center of the ball to create a hollow space in the center. This will push the dough up above the edges around the perimeter of the mold. Roughly shape about a tablespoon of date paste into a ball and drop it into the hollowed space. Use the displaced dough from around the edges of the mold cavity to enclose the date ball, covering it completely. Smooth the dough flat.

8. Turn the mold face down and tap the top corner of the mold head firmly on the work surface (whack!) once or twice to release the cookie. Carefully transfer the cookie to the prepared baking sheet and place them 1-inch apart.

9. To shape maamoul by hand: Dust your work surface with flour. Use your hand or a rolling pin dusted with flour to flatten the dough ball to about ¼-inch thick in an oblong shape, about 2 ½-inches long by 1 ½-inches wide. Shape a tablespoon of date paste into a log similar in shape but smaller than the flattened dough. Lay the log of date paste in the center of the dough and cover the date filling by enclosing it in the dough and sealing the edges together up over the date paste log. Turn the log over, continuing to smooth and shape the dough by hand into a log, ensuring there are no cracks. Use a fork to press or a strawberry huller to pinch the top of the dough in a deep, decorative pattern, piercing all the way to the

date filling. Carefully transfer the cookies to the prepared baking sheets and place them 1 inch apart.

10. Shape the cookies: Repeat the shaping process with a mold or by hand with the rest of the dough and date filling.

11. Bake the cookies: Bake the cookies, one sheet pan at a time, in the center of the oven, for 15-17 minutes, or until the cookies are a pale golden brown. Check the cookies frequently in the last 5 minutes of cook time to check for cracking. If the tops begin to crack, immediately remove the cookies from the oven.

12. Cool and serve the cookies: Allow the cookies to cool completely, undisturbed, on the pan, at least one hour. Sift confectioners' sugar over the cookies and give them a fresh dusting again just before serving.

13. To store the cookies: Store the cookies in an airtight container for up to two weeks at room temperature, or for two months frozen.

Nutritional Value (Amount per Serving):

Calories: 205; Fat: 8.75; Carb: 29.81; Protein: 3.04

Turkish Delight (Lokum)

Prep Time: 20 Minutes
Cook Time: 25 Minutes
Serves: 50

Ingredients:

- or Dusting And Coating:
- 3 ½ tablespoons powdered sugar
- 3 ½ tablespoons cornstarch
- or The Turkish Delight:
- 3 cups superfine or baker's sugar
- 1 ¾ cups cold water
- 1 medium lemon, juiced
- ½ cup cold water
- ½ cup + 2 tablespoons cornstarch
- 4 ¾ tablespoons powdered gelatin
- 1 ½ teaspoons rose water
- 1 to 2 drops red food coloring, optional
- Gold edible glitter, optional

Directions:

1. Prepare the baking dish: Line an 8 x 8-inch square baking dish with plastic wrap or parchment paper.
2. Make the dusting mixture: Into a small bowl, combine 3 ½ tablespoons powdered sugar and 3 ½ tablespoons cornstarch. Sprinkle about 2 teaspoons of this mixture over the base and sides of the baking dish. Set the remaining dusting mixture aside.
3. Make the sugar syrup: Into a large saucepan set over medium-low heat, add the superfine sugar, lemon juice and 1 ¾ cups water. Heat gently until the sugar is completely dissolved – do not boil or even simmer.
4. In a small bowl, combine ½ cup plus 2 tablespoons cornstarch with ½ cup cold water. Whisk into sugar syrup. Sprinkle the gelatin over the sugar

syrup and whisk to break up any lumps. Bring to a boil (you want the liquid to reach 250°F with a candy thermometer), then simmer over a medium heat for 20 minutes, whisking often. The mixture is ready when it thickens and turns pale yellow – like a soft jelly that is just about set.

5. Flavor and set the candy: Remove from the heat and set aside for 5 minutes. Stir in the rose water and 1 to 2 drops of red food coloring. (If using chopped nuts, stir them in now.) Pour the mixture into the prepared dish.

6. Leave it to set up in a cool place on your countertop overnight. Ten to 12 hours is ideal, but if you'd like it to set even more you can leave it for up to 24 hours.

7. Cut the Turkish delight: Dust a cutting board with some of the reserved dusting mixture, and then invert the Turkish delight onto it. Remove the dish; peel off the parchment. Use a long sharp knife or a bench scraper to cut straight down from top to bottom. Do not drag the knife through the candy to cut into cubes. Once cut, roll each cube gently in the dusting mixture to coat.

8. Decorate with glitter: If using, go ahead and sprinkle the edible glitter over the Turkish delight.

9. Dry the Turkish delight: Line a baking sheet with parchment paper. Place the Turkish delight cubes in a single on the tray with a little space between each cube. Let the Turkish delight air dry for 24 hours to prevent homemade Turkish delight from sweating. Sprinkle the remaining cornstarch mixture over the candy to gently coat each piece and leave it uncovered on your countertop. Once it's dried for 24 hours Turkish delight is ready to eat. The texture is somewhat between a homemade marshmallow and soft jelly.

10. Enjoy and store: Homemade Turkish delight is best enjoyed when fresh, though it keeps well stored in a dry place for up to 1 month. Layer the candy between sheets of parchment in an airtight container on your countertop in a cool, dry place away from light and heat. Make sure there is a little space between each piece of Turkish delight.

Nutritional Value (Amount per Serving):

Calories: 76; Fat: 1.62; Carb: 8.76; Protein: 8.72

Baklava Cheesecake

Prep Time: 30 Minutes
Cook Time: 1 Hour 30 Minutes
Serves: 16

Ingredients:

- or The Phyllo Crust
- Extra virgin olive oil
- ⅓cup walnuts, chopped
- ⅓cup pistachios, chopped
- 2 tablespoons sugar
- 1 teaspoon ground cinnamon
- 10 sheets phyllo dough, thawed
- or The Cheesecake Batter
- 3 pounds whole milk ricotta cheese, strained and room temperature
- 8 large eggs, room temperature
- 1 ¼ cup sugar
- 1 teaspoon vanilla extract
- Zest of 2 large oranges, divided
- or Garnish
- ¼ to ⅓cup honey, warmed
- More chopped walnuts and pistachios

Directions:

1. Heat the oven to 350°F and position a rack in the middle.
2. Prepare a 10-inch springform cake pan and brush the sides and bottom with the olive oil. Place the pan on the center of a large sheetpan.
3. Make the nut mixture: In a small bowl, mix together the nuts, sugar, and cinnamon. Set aside for now.
4. Assemble the phyllo crust: Lay two sheets of phyllo in the oiled springform pan and press gently onto the bottom and sides. Brush the phyllo with extra virgin olive oil, including any parts hanging over the pan. Lay another

3 sheets of phyllo on top so they overlap, rotating the pan so that the phyllo will cover it on all sides (there should be phyllo slack hanging over on all sides of the pan). Brush with olive oil, then sprinkle the nut mixture over the phyllo to cover the bottom of the pan. Place the remaining phyllo sheets over the nut mixture, following the same pattern and making sure to brush each sheet of phyllo with extra virgin olive oil. (If the overlay of phyllo dough is too long, you can fold it over or cut it with a pair of kitchen scissors).

5. Prepare the cheesecake batter: In the bowl of a standing mixer fitted with a paddle attachment, add the cheese, eggs, sugar, vanilla extract, and half the orange zest. Start the mixer on low for 1 to 2 minutes then increase the speed to medium-low (2 on the KitchenAid mixer) for 10 minutes. The mixture will look light and fluffy. If using a hand-mixer, keep the speed low. If using a wooden spoon, mix continuously until fluffy.

6. Assemble and bake the baklava cheesecake: Pour the batter into the prepared pan with the phyllo.

7. Bake: Place the cheesecake in a preheated oven for one to 1 ½ hours or until the batter has mostly firmed up and the top of the cake and phyllo crust has gained a nice golden brown color. The batter may still jiggle slightly in the middle, but it will firm up once cooled. (Do keep an eye on the phyllo crust, and if it is turning too brown too quickly, you may need to adjust the heat down to 325°F).

8. Cool: Remove from the oven and place on a wire rack to cool for 1 to 2 hours. Transfer to the fridge for at least 6 hours or up to overnight.

9. Release from the pan: Break off any extra phyllo crust hanging over the sides that could make it difficult to release the cake. (You can crumble the crust and add it on top to garnish). Release the lever on the side of the pan, remove the cake and transfer to a platter.

10. Garnish and serve: Add chopped nuts and remaining orange zest to the top of the cake for garnish. Warm the honey and drizzle it all over the crust and top of the cake.

Nutritional Value (Amount per Serving):

Calories: 328; Fat: 18.06; Carb: 29.02; Protein: 13.23

CONCLUSION

In conclusion, the Mediterranean Refresh diet is a healthy eating pattern that emphasizes whole, minimally processed foods and healthy fats. This diet is rich in nutrients, antioxidants, and anti-inflammatory compounds that can help support overall health and wellbeing, while also reducing the risk of chronic diseases, such as heart disease, diabetes, and certain types of cancer.

The Mediterranean Refresh diet offers a wide range of benefits, including improved heart health, weight management, reduced inflammation, improved gut health, and improved cognitive function. This diet may also support healthy aging, improve mood, support fertility, promote sustainable and environmentally-friendly food choices, and offer potential benefits for skin health, sleep quality, and athletic performance.

Overall, the Mediterranean Refresh diet is a delicious and satisfying way to support overall health and wellbeing, while also promoting sustainable and environmentally-friendly food choices. By emphasizing whole, nutrient-dense foods and minimizing the consumption of processed and animal-based foods, individuals can support their overall health while enjoying a wide variety of delicious and nutritious foods.

APPENDIX RECIPE INDEX

Made in the USA
Las Vegas, NV
20 September 2023